Magic in the Muck

finding grace in chaos

May you find moments of grace + magic in every part of your life!

Jennifer Nagel

JENNIFER NAGEL, MA, RCC

Published by Grace in Chaos Publications, April, 2018
ISBN: 9781775308409

Editor: Karen Melin
Typeset: Greg Salisbury
Book Cover Design: Judith Mazari
Portrait Photographer: Daniel Sicolo

DISCLAIMER: This is a personal work of non-fiction. Some of the names and identifying details have been changed to protect the privacy of individuals. Readers of this publication agree that neither Jennifer Nagel, nor her publisher will be held responsible or liable for damages that may be alleged as resulting directly or indirectly from the use of this publication. Neither the publisher nor the author can be held accountable for the information provided by, or actions, resulting from, accessing these resources. This book is not intended in any way to replace other professional healthcare or mental health advise, but to support it.

To:

My husband Rod,

who has always supported my dreams with unconditional love and encouragement

and to

my children, Mahalia and Kai,

who teach me every day about what it means to show up.

Table of Contents

Foreword

This book captures key concepts for living a healthy emotional life and engages the reader in understanding and applying these concepts to their own life. The author, Jennifer Nagel, is a seasoned psychotherapist who explains the concepts by using metaphors and sharing deeply moving personal examples. It is so engaging that there are times when you feel as though you are reading a novel.

Incorporated into the book are many of the universal concepts taught by the world famous therapist, Virginia Satir. However, Nagel has done so by using her own language and wisdom. She creates new language for teaching the importance of "becoming aware," inviting you to be present and "show up" to your life, embracing the fullness of your experience including your joys and your sorrows.

The author then guides the reader on the various ways that one can "show up" to oneself, such as acknowledging one's emotions, identifying any judgments about those emotions and releasing the judgment, questioning perceptions and expectations that may no longer be helpful, and identifying underlying yearnings.

In addition to helping people know how they can "show up" to embrace their life more fully, the author breaks new ground with her proposal that there is a "Universal Container" that holds space for every one of us on this planet and holds us with love and acceptance. Other theorists have referred to this energy space as the "Life Force" or "Spirit," but by naming it "the Great Container," the author re-expands our understanding of this energy. She likens it to a set of Russian dolls whereby the life energy becomes a container at all the various levels of humanity from the individual to all in the universe. And, finally, she describes it as going beyond the universe and connecting us with the Divine.

As a seasoned therapist myself, I have understood the importance of creating a "container," where the client(s) could be safe to grow and heal, but with Nagel's describing "life energy" as a container, we are offered a new way of understanding how it is "holding" us with love and acceptance at all the levels of our human existence.

Sharon Loeschen, Licensed Clinical Social Worker

Author of "The Satir Process" and "Enriching Your Relationship with Yourself and Others"

If you feel lost, disappointed, hesitant, or weak, return to yourself,

to who you are, here and now and when you get there,

you will discover yourself, like a lotus flower in full bloom,

even in a muddy pond, beautiful and strong.

Masaru Emoto, Secret Life of Water

Introducing Moments of Grace

What are moments of grace? They are those moments that find their way into our lives in the midst of chaos that offer reprieve from the storm; the small miracles that connect one breath to the next. We recognize them immediately, yet do not always stop to appreciate them — to notice them and see them for what they are. Moments when the mountain doesn't seem so daunting. Or moments to recognize what is happening, to pause, or simply to breathe.

To fully experience and appreciate these moments of grace, we must fully experience and embrace life. This means we also need to fully experience and embrace the pain. It is through embracing the pain that we are most able to find those moments of grace.

It was May, 2007 as I was just starting my second trimester of pregnancy with our first child. The excitement, nervousness, and anticipation of becoming parents was beginning to feel real. We were only half a year away from a new adventure and challenge and together, my husband and I could not have felt more enthusiastic. That anticipation and excitement turned to fear and dread when the doctor told my husband that he had cancer. Stage 4 Non-Hodgkins Lymphoma with merely weeks to live. What?! This was not part of our plan. We had not anticipated something like cancer getting in the way of experiencing the journey of becoming parents together. I remember so clearly sitting in the chair at the doctor's office, pen and notepaper in hand to take copious amounts of notes (my way of coping with holding back the flood of emotions that were building inside of me), and Rod's question of "What happens after Stage 4?" that prompted my whispered answer to myself, "There is no after Stage 4."

Breathing in, breathing out. Focusing on my breath. Focusing on this new life growing inside of me with the knowledge that my stress and anxiety would have an impact on my body and the baby's. And yet, there was a deeper part within me that knew the strength within Rod. I had such a moment of pride for him when he told the doctor that he had gone for a 10 kilometre run the day before. The doctor's jaw literally dropped as he said he did not know how that was humanly possible given the results of the scans and what they were seeing inside his body.

Maybe that was a defining moment of grace for me too; the knowledge that the human spirit, my husband's spirit, could out-ride and override the human body. If the fact that he had run for 10 kilometres the day before he learned that he had Stage 4 cancer could defy any rational explanation by the doctors, then maybe there was more hope than we were being presented at that moment.

Moments of grace. We went straight from the doctor's office to our favourite forest for a walk amongst the trees. Something about being in nature, being together, alone with our thoughts and fears but together in our facing what this all might mean created a hint of ease. As we were walking, Rod shared his fears about what would happen to us. I knew at a very cellular level that whatever the outcome was, I was not going to go anywhere and our relationship would be stronger, closer, and deeper than ever before.

The moments of terror at times were overwhelming. Times of darkness and secret fears unshared for want of not giving any momentum to those thoughts. But they were there. What would it mean to have a baby in the midst of grieving the loss of my husband? The only way to face this for me was to literally be in the *now*. I couldn't allow myself to think about what might occur. My mantra became "at *this* moment in time…" At this moment in time, my husband is alive. At this moment in time, we are enjoying one another. At this moment in time, there are other options and treatments to try. At this moment in time, there is still hope. At this moment in time, we are surrounded by a community of people who love us and care for us. At this moment in time. Moment by moment, we could do this.

We journeyed through four rounds of experimental chemotherapy treatments, through extended months' long hospital stays while I continued to work full-time and our baby continued to grow inside me preparing to grace the world with her presence.

Our daughter's middle name is Grace. She is named for the multitude of moments we had along the way, including the moments surrounding her birth. Her due date was the beginning of November but Rod was due back in the hospital towards the end of October for full body radiation and a stem cell transplant from an unrelated donor. By the way, if you are into statistics, it was a medically perfect match, with the doctors pegging the odds at one in eight million! The thought of him not being present for the birth of our child was painfully sad and anxiety-provoking for me. We had hired a doula, along with our wonderful team of midwives, for my own emotional support in the birth process. Rod and I joked about choosing the arrival date for our baby. October 18 seemed like a good day because that would allow him to be present for the grand arrival right before his return to the hospital.

October 18 became part of our everyday talk and somewhat of a mantra. We were telling everyone, including the midwives when our baby would be born, knowing full well that planning the exact date of arrival was not really in our control. Yet I talked to our baby. I talked to God. I talked to my body. I let go of the expectation but held onto the hope. On October 18 my water broke, contractions began, our daughter was born and Rod was there for all of it! A miraculous moment of grace — enjoying our own birth into parenthood and witnessing the amazing miracle of welcoming a new being into our lives.

But moments of grace are also defined by the other moments; the chaos, the ugliness, the terror, the anger and resentment, and all the stuff that is difficult to fully face. Without those moments we would not know what grace is. The gift of Rod being present for the birth of our daughter, and given an extra day home from the hospital (where the nurses recorded him as having checked in otherwise he would have lost his hospital bed) eventually led to the day he actually had to return for what was the 'last hope' of his treatment and another lengthy stay in the hospital.

I spiralled into despair and fear — probably enhanced by hormonal changes — and postpartum depression hit me hard. While I was pregnant I had been able to be fully present with Rod when I was with him at the hospital. Having a newborn meant my attention could no longer be fully on my husband. There was a baby that literally needed me more than my husband did.

Moments of grace: my mother showing up for me in a way that went well beyond the call of duty, the moments of peace while breastfeeding in the still and silent hours of the middle of the night rocking in the gliding chair. Continuing the process of being in the moment. Being in the now. Riding the waves of emotion without judgment.

This is not to say that there was not judgment. Oh, there was judgment alright — my own judgments about my ability as a parent, my abilities as a human being. But I kept learning to come back to centre. Coming back to my Self — my whole, complete, and more-than-enough Self. Embracing and appreciating the moments where kindness or sleep or silence or support or connection offered reprieve, but also learning to embrace and come to appreciate the moments that were far from grace-filled.

How do we identify the moments of grace? I believe these moments are ever-present when we really pay attention. Staying present in the moment may not be easy to do. Very often we are focused on what has already happened in the past, what might happen or what needs to happen in the future; the "shoulds", "should haves" and "should be" rather than the "what is". If we are able to stay present in this very moment — and this means being present for the not-so-pleasant moments too — we will find those moments of grace. Moments of grace, moments of awe, moments of beauty, moments of chaos, moments of transformation. All of these seconds of experience that, when added up, equal our own unique and one-of-a-kind lives.

This book is an exploration of what we all go through in the process of change. Change is inevitable, and how we face or don't face this has a tremendous impact on the degree to which we show up for Life. What are the conditions that we need to cultivate within and around us in order to fully show up and live Life out? How do we get through — and out of — the muck of feeling stuck and blocked from knowing what to do next? And how do we truly discover and embrace the magic, the Grace, that exists within the muck itself?

The **drive for order interrupts** the **beautiful chaos** needed for **creativity** to thrive. - Simon Sinek

1

The Status Quo

Have you ever noticed that you tend to prefer things to be somewhat predictable in your life? It is much easier to stick with what is familiar and comfortable than to venture into unknown territory. Maybe you do like taking risks and trying new things, but as soon as it gets a little bit too scary and foreign you fall back to what is safe and familiar. We tend to live in a status quo, for this is what gives structure and predictability to our lives. Status quo is defined as "the existing state of affairs." In other words, the way things are. We like things to be the way they have existed. We like to think we can predict how someone will respond or react to something you say or do, like thinking your friends will laugh at a joke you tell them or predicting that your partner will be angry that you are running late or that your mother will be worried if you don't phone her on a regular basis. The status quo may be comfortable because it is what we know from our own experience and our own relationships with others.

However, if you really allow yourself to stop and think about it, we often want something different or something more in our lives. We might not even know what that "something different" might be, only that we are not happy with the way things are and feel stuck in it. This can create a tension between the desire for safety and predictability, and the desire to take some risks for something new and different. Sometimes Life has a way of surprising us when we least expect it and in ways that we could not possibly have planned or predicted. Maybe your partner is calm and supportive when you predicted he or she would freak out that you lost something important, or maybe someone reacts in anger to something you said when you truly have no clue about what caused their strong reaction. The world is unpredictable and it is inevitable that we will get knocked right out of our comfortable (but not necessarily pleasant) status quo and into the zone of the unknown.

Impacts from our histories that have not been dealt with also have a way of coming along and sabotaging our relationships with ourselves and others. For example, what if I have not resolved my old insecurities about being liked and accepted by others, but I have managed to put those insecurities aside when all is safe and predictable in my world? I would then most likely be triggered by somebody else's criticisms of me or by my perceptions of their judgments when safety and predictability are threatened. This can then impact my own judgments of myself as well as how I interact with others.

THE OBSTACLE COURSE AND ITS TRIGGERS

Let's face it — life is not a smooth ride for the majority of people. It's not always easy to show up at one hundred percent. Life is kind of like an obstacle course as we navigate through relationships with family, friends, lovers, colleagues and acquaintances. We can become blocked in the flow of our lives and stuck in old patterns that we do not even know we have. In fact, we may not even realize they are patterns at all and might assume it is actually 'just who we are' and part of our personality. We may not even have the slightest idea that we can possibly change these patterns of ours. When we are blocked or stuck we stop fully living and experiencing life, and it can seem as though we are dying a little on the inside.

Experiencing the Muck

Getting stuck in the muck of it all (or not even realizing that we are deep in the thick of it) happens to everyone at one point or another. Everyone has his or her way of dealing with it. For some, it is a matter of not dealing with it at all and avoiding any kind of conflict or flooding of emotions. For others it's all about fighting and survival at any cost, or about trying to make some kind of rational sense and explanation of what the muck might mean. What about the idea of actually growing and learning from our experience of the muck? This would mean allowing ourselves to truly sit in it and with it and allow the full experience to bring us to a whole new level of awareness and growth. To detoxify the emotional and mental baggage that we no longer need to carry in our lives we need to allow this muck to come to the surface and be set free. There will be grief, there will be anger, and there will be hurt, guilt, and shame. And there will be more. Allow all of it to be there, knowing that this conglomerate of emotions will absolutely shift and change, for it is in the acknowledging of the muck and the crap that we can begin to set it all free.

Life can certainly feel like an obstacle course at times with challenges and road blocks that seem to prevent us from moving forward. And then, just as we are making progress something comes along that we could not possibly expect and we are triggered into some kind of reacting with anger, hurt, fear, confusion, surprise or some other emotion. Our physiology shifts into fight, flight or freeze mode and we experience chaos.

We can be triggered when something or someone reminds us of a past experience or a relative or somebody we know. We can react in a way that might have no bearing on the context but we are somehow reminded of a similar situation or interaction from the past. For example, your boss reprimands you for not finishing a report on time and suddenly you are reacting the way you did when you were scolded by your mother as a child, or you are suddenly flooded with anxiety and fears of not being good enough, or your anger and blame gets triggered and you become defensive with your boss. Initially, these reactions and associations with past impacts are out of your conscious awareness. If you allow yourself to reflect on what just happened you might discover a connection with a similar past experience.

WHERE DO THESE REACTIONS AND TRIGGERS COME FROM?

We all prefer things to be predictable in our lives as predictability allows us to feel some level of safety. Most of the time, we are not even consciously aware of our assumptions because when our expectations are met we do not notice them. For example, when you leave your house for work or school in the morning you most likely assume it will still be standing there when you get home at the end of the day. When you start your car engine, you expect it to simply start running. You only notice your expectations when they are not being met. When the engine does not start. When you lose your home. When you are not getting your needs met. When you are young you learn how to get your needs met by your parents or guardians. If and when these needs are met consistently over time, you learn what you need to do or how you need to be to get those needs met. This is how you are safe at a very fundamental level of survival.

While predictability allows us to experience safety, the fact is that we are born into an unpredictable world. Think of it — after nine months in the warm darkness of the womb you suddenly have this experience of new physical sensations, of moving through the birth canal or being removed from the womb, of the cool air on your skin for the first time, your first breath, your first cry; so many firsts that you could not have predicted. As you continue to experience the moments of your life, you also encounter how you are cared for or not cared for by your parents or guardians. You experience yourself through your parents' eyes, voice, touch and actions that communicate how they are experiencing you. This has a tremendous impact on your identity. Your body has a physiological response to every experience. It might be a startle response, or a sensation in your stomach, head, chest, arms, or anywhere in your body. You take in information with all of your senses even when you are not conscious of doing so — how you are touched, what you see, hear, smell, taste — and you receive so much information energetically from your environment and relationships.

Messages Of Our Emotions

As you experience physiological responses in your body, you also have emotions. Your emotions are another source of information available to you that have positive intentions and messages for you if you pay attention. What does your anger tell you about what you deserve to have at a moment that you are not getting? Are you needing to be heard? To be acknowledged? To belong? To be loved? To be safe? To be free? When these universal needs are not being met, they give rise to emotions such as anger, sadness, fear, and anxiety. What about when you have joy, what is it telling you? If you learn to really listen to the deeper intentions of what your emotions are telling you, you might realize that all of your emotions are important. We learn to judge them as good or bad by the way emotions are handled within the families we grew up, but when we can listen to their positive intentions, we can also learn to accept all of our emotions as part of our human experience.

The Meanings We Make Belong To Us

As human beings, we are a meaning-making species. We make meanings out of whatever is occurring in our lives. If we are startled by a loud sound, one of the emotions that might come up for us is fear, and we automatically start making meanings out of what might be going on. Or somebody says something to you and there is something about the tone in which they said it that leads you to read between the lines and make all kinds of possible interpretations about what they may have meant. The meanings that we make come from our own personal histories and how we have stored those memories within us. The exact same sound or incident can elicit completely different responses from people depending on their histories and the context.

I remember sitting in a meeting in China where some of the people in the room were from North America and others were from Asia. There was a series of loud popping sounds from outside and the people from North America all had startle reflex reactions and an initial fear response whereas those from Asia remained calm and seemed confused by our reactions. What some of us were interpreting as the sound of gunshots was celebratory fireworks in honour of some festival that was occurring at the time. The Asian members of our group were very familiar with the tradition of fireworks, whereas the North Americans were not expecting any loud fireworks in the middle of the day and had no context for the festival's customs. This was such a clear example of how associations get made from our own personal life experiences.

Decisions For Survival

Whatever meaning you hold determines the conscious or unconscious decisions you make about what you need to do to survive and be safe. Whether you freeze and take shelter, run away, engage in conflict and fighting, or put your own needs aside in order to please others and protect your relationship, your decisions become your truth and you will unconsciously live out that truth until it enters your awareness. When you are young, the meanings you make are entirely about you. You might see or hear your parents arguing and the fight may have nothing at all to do with you but you are unable to understand that. Because you don't understand that other people's actions are not about you, you make meanings such as It's all my fault that they are fighting" or "If only I had hugged mom when she came home, then she would be happy and they wouldn't be fighting right now." You might make a decision such as: "I will do whatever it takes to keep people happy." This becomes a pattern of survival which might show up in the form of sacrificing your own needs or your own opinions for the sake of keeping the peace, always giving to others to the point of your own exhaustion, and going above and beyond in meeting others' expectations because you might believe this is the only way they will like you and accept you. If you grow up without realizing this decision you made when you were little, you might be so very tired from trying to keep everyone happy, unable to take good care of your own needs but doing so much to take care of everyone else's. Or if people are in conflict and arguing with one another you might be triggered and filled with anxiety so you bend over backwards to keep the peace no matter what. This is just one example of how a pattern of survival is formed. To quote Virginia Satir, "It is not about what happens to you, it is about what you *do* with what happens to

8

you." It is about the meanings that you form, the emotional responses that you have, and the subconscious decisions that you make. Every one of us has multiple survival patterns and most are out of our awareness. The key word here is survival, and survival is about the intention to stay alive. What becomes costly and painful is when these patterns use up much of our energy and block us from fully experiencing our lives in the present.

Your Survival Energy Patterns

Here is a clue for you to know if you are using one of your survival energy patterns: if you are having a reaction, if you feel triggered in any way, if your frustration or anger lasts for more than a few seconds, it is linked to some kind of unfinished business and energy pattern from the past. Knowing this, you can ask yourself: "What is happening for me right now in my experience? How am I feeling? What are the meanings I am making right now? Where do these meanings come from? Are they familiar to me?" Simply by asking yourself some of these questions, you start to reflect on your experience. When you reflect on your experience you already begin to change the brain. The results of modern research on neuroplasticity show that our life experiences literally change the brain. You can become more fully aware of your experience. Awareness allows you to more conscientiously choose what you want to shift and change, even when you may not be certain of how you will do it. Knowing you want something different opens the door to showing up for possibilities. You can accept your past experiences without needing them to rule your life. You can live and respond in the present instead of dwelling and reacting in the past. Acceptance does not mean you have to like it. Acceptance means it is what it is — it has happened, it is happening, and you have choice in how you respond.

ACCEPTANCE AND CHOICES

When my husband and I received the news of his cancer diagnosis, there was nothing to like about that. It was a blow that was wildly unexpected and seemed to sneak up on us in the most unpredictable of ways. The scans and test results were undeniable and it was clear that we could not change what was happening in that moment in time. The work we faced was about accepting what was happening and choosing what we were going to do about that. Rod knew what he was dealing with: stage 4 cancer. He accepted that he had cancer, but he decided that he was not going to allow himself to be defined by the disease.

Acceptance also did not do anything to interfere with his determination and his very, very stubborn nature. To give you a sense of just how strong his will was, he was the guy on the exercise bike in his hospital wing while undergoing chemotherapy. He was the guy who refused to wear a hospital gown the entire time he was in the hospital because he did not want to give any credibility or weight to the story of being sick. He was the guy who refused to let any hospital porters wheel him to any tests or medical procedures, in spite of it being hospital policy.

I remember when he went to get his Hickman line inserted at the beginning of all his treatments. That particular procedure involved minor surgery that consisted of inserting a catheter right by the right atrium of his heart into the Superior Vena Cava. Once that

Hickman line was in, it would allow the chemo drugs to be administered directly into his cardiovascular system, as well as drawing blood for various tests and analyses without the need to repeatedly poke and prod him with countless needles.

When the time came for the procedure, a poor unsuspecting hospital porter showed up with a wheeled gurney, thinking that he would be wheeling some sick, weak cancer patient into surgery. Nope. Rod took one look at the gurney, adamantly declared that he would walk to the operating room, and just started striding out of the room. The baffled and confused porter had no choice but to chase him out, wheeling an empty gurney.

That was not the end of it. When the surgery was done (it was surprisingly minor, essentially day surgery), Rod apparently grew bored of waiting for the porter for the return trip. His IV drip was empty, the Hickman line was securely installed, and there was no point in waiting. He made the decision to walk back by himself.

I recall that I was feeing a bit anxious and concerned as I wondered why it was taking so long for Rod to get back to his room. I was at the front desk of the ward talking to the nurses who were all so amazing and supportive, all of us collectively wondering where Rod had gotten to, when all of a sudden the ward's automatic doors burst open, and in strolled Rod with an empty IV bag slung nonchalantly over one shoulder.

And for just about all of the treatments from that time forward, Rod simply refused to be ported anywhere on anything with wheels. He continued to accept whatever was happening with the cancer and his treatments without ever giving up on his determination to keep on living. He continued to make the decision to live. I accepted that determination of his whole-heartedly!

DECIDING HOW AND WHERE TO FOCUS YOUR ENERGY

You can decide how and where to focus your energy at a moment in time. Remembering that you are human and that you will inevitably get triggered at times, it is possible to become more consciously aware of when this is happening. You can remember to breathe — the way we breathe has an impact on our physiological response and can truly shift us out of a place of unease and discomfort. You can notice that you have had a reaction and pause briefly to pay attention to that awareness. Taking a moment to be curious about your reaction means noticing your feelings, thoughts, expectations, and deeper yearnings that are occurring. What are the deeper needs that you are trying to get met at that moment in time? You can ascertain whether the need is for connection, love, intimacy, belonging, acknowledgment, safety or whatever it may be. You can then make a choice to shelve it for exploration and processing later if needed, or you can do something right then and there if it is necessary.

And yes, there will be moments when you are triggered into chaos and everything may seem completely out of control, knocking you right out of your predictable status quo into new and unknown territory.

QUESTIONS FOR REFLECTION

This is the first of a series of questions in this book. The space provided is for you to begin the process of your own reflection. I invite you to write, draw, or colour in this space, and to also journal so that you may go deeper with your reflections.

1. **What are some of your expectations?**
   For example: I expect myself to remain calm in the face of chaos.
   I expect myself to be aware of my reactions and to be able to change them.
   I expect my children to listen to me and respond when I am asking them to do something.
   I expect my husband to understand me. I expect to be on time for appointments and meetings.

2. **What happens when your expectations are not met?**
   For example: When my children do not listen to me, I have feelings of frustration and anger. If I am not experiencing calm in chaos, I might have fear, anger, and guilt. I become reactive and then experience guilt and shame about some of my reactions because "I should know better" (another expectation).

3. What else triggers you? Or in other words, what else do you react to?

For example: I get triggered sometimes when there is conflict or if I experience myself being blamed for something I did not do. My guilt and shame can get triggered when something I say is misinterpreted and taken the wrong way. Any anger directed straight at me impacts me at the physiological level first – an internal startle, raised body temperature, heart beating faster.

4. Where and how has this shown up in your life in the past?

For example: When I was a child, I remember feeling very uncomfortable and upset, and sometimes afraid of other people's anger even when it was not directed towards me. I would want to keep the peace between my parents when they were arguing, and would do the same with my peers in school as well. I also remember feeling invisible at times when I tried to speak up in groups (such as large extended family gatherings) and either could not get a word in or nobody seemed to hear me trying to talk.

5. What are some of the common themes of these triggers?

For example: When I look at the triggers I have used as examples, I see themes of being triggered by not being heard and not being understood. There is also a common theme around what happens for me when there is conflict and my desire to avoid it altogether.

6. As you become aware of some of your triggers and how you react to them, what would you like to change?

For example: I would like to change my reactivity towards others when they express their anger and frustration towards me. I would like to continue working on my patience and acceptance of myself and of others.

7. **What would you need to resolve or let go of for that to change?**

For example: When I reflect on my responses to the previous questions, I become aware that I need to work on letting go of some of my expectations, as well as changing some of them. This does not mean letting go of them in resignation. I can let go of them with more acceptance and acknowledge that I do not need to keep holding onto them if they are going to hold me back. I need to let go of the expectation for my children to get along harmoniously 24 hours a day, 7 days a week (because we KNOW that just is not a reality for ANY of us to get along harmoniously 24/7 so how could I expect that of my children?). I also need to resolve my own hurt and disappointment when not heard or understood by those I care about and love the most in my life.

8. **Are you ready to work on this?**

You do not need to know 'the how' part yet. At this point all you need to do is check in with yourself to see if you are connecting with the idea of working on change within yourself. A yes or no answer is all that is needed here and there is no right or wrong answer. A 'no' simply means there are some blocks that may need to be looked at and tended to first. Fear can be a block. A 'yes' answer means "YES, I am ready to do the work. Let's do this!"

There are some things you **learn best in calm**, and some in storm.

- Anais Nin

2

Encountering Chaos

Chaos is an inevitable part of everyone's life. Some people do seem to encounter a great deal more chaos than others while others seem to have an abundance of resilience, but we all experience chaos. Let's face it, chaos does not feel good. The unpredictability, the unknown, the loss, the pain, the craziness of it all can instil all kinds of anxiety and fear. Yet as Virginia Satir has said: Chaos is essential for change. We get triggered into chaos when something happens that is not within our current status quo or familiar comfort zone. For example, your partner decides to leave the marriage, somebody you love dies, the doctor tells you that you have cancer, you move to a new neighbourhood or a new city, you start a new job, you get fired from your job, or basically anything that puts you in the realm of the unfamiliar, the unpredictable, and the unknown. The twilight zone can be a scary place to be. Encountering chaos can be confusing, devastating, gut-wrenching, and completely beyond the realm of understanding. The circumstances may be way beyond our control, our emotions are in over-drive, and we can be completely overwhelmed in the midst of it all.

CHAOS WITHIN YOURSELF VS. CHAOS AROUND YOU

I want to differentiate between the experience of chaos within yourself and the experience of chaos around you. You very well might be able to remain calm in the midst of a storm all around you. Others might be in a state of chaos while you can be centred and present for it all. Then again, the chaos around you might trigger your own internal hurricane. Our chaos is a reflection of how we are processing and reacting to what is going on within us and/or around us. Encounters with chaos can be — and usually are — completely unpredictable and are not necessarily the result of some huge catastrophic event. Most often, our tendency might be to try our hardest to avoid chaos altogether.

Yet, if chaos is essential for change it means we have to have it — all of it — for change to take place. Now this is where it can get tricky. Our Western medical system does not like chaos. Chaos gets medicated. I am not saying that there is not a place for medicine as I do believe that it is necessary at times. However, I also believe that there are many incidences of prescriptions being handed out for what I would call a normal response to the circumstances. We don't like chaos. We run away from it. We hide from it. We avoid it. If we medicate chaos we medicate the opportunity for change, and if chaos is essential for change we need to learn to be in it, to go through it, and to get to the other side. We need to truly know and have hope that we will not remain in this state forever.

ᕗᴄCASE EXAMPLE: "ALAN"ᕤ

I had a client who had been dealing with clinical depression for over 25 years. Alan had been on a variety of medications, had experiences with hospitalization, and had even undergone electro-convulsive shock therapy treatment. Nothing was truly working for him and the doctors were basically telling him that he would be stuck with this mental illness for the rest of his life. He had accepted this as his status quo and the only reason he was coming for therapy was in the context of family therapy to help his daughters with some other issues that were happening.

Alan had been prevented from experiencing his own chaos. In an effort to help with his depression, the treatments he had received supported him not being thrown into the chaos, wherein change can emerge.

Do you want to know what triggered him into chaos? When we looked at the idea of depression being a solution to a problem and, if it was a solution, then we needed to be curious about whatever the problem was that depression was trying to solve. This new way of looking at the depression put him in a struggle between what he had believed to be true about the life sentence of his condition, and the new possibility that perhaps the depression could change if the root problem was identified and resolved.

The chaos served to lessen the numbness he had been experiencing. Now he could have anxiety, excitement, hope, fear, guilt and shame all at the same time. I am quite sure this was not the most comfortable of experiences for him, but it launched a whole new energy into exploring his relationship with his past and how it was impacting his present-day relationships with his wife and children. From this new experience of chaos, he could be in touch with the pain and loss around not fully living that the depression had constituted, and he could also be in touch with new hope and possibilities for himself. He could make new decisions for consciously being more present for his family and he even started being more spontaneous with them which, up until that point, had been completely out of his family's experience of him and came as such a pleasant surprise to his wife and children.

When we allow ourselves to show up and experience the chaos, our relationship with the past can be transformed and we can be open to new possibilities for living life more fully in the present.

QUESTIONS FOR REFLECTION

1. **How do you experience chaos when it comes up for you?**

   For example: When I experience chaos, I notice my heart racing, my thoughts become scattered initially, I feel stressed along with either anger or fear or both, I see myself as out of control and overwhelmed with the unpredictability of whatever is going on. I might initially freeze as I experience myself as stuck and unable to initially have any sense of what to do in the situation.

2. **Think of a time recently when you experienced some chaos, even if it was for only a brief amount of time (e.g., somebody cut you off in traffic, or you had an argument with someone you care about, or your children were not listening to you, or you received an unexpected bill in the mail, or basically anything you had a reaction to). What was it that you were needing and wanting at that moment in time?**

   For example: When I sit with the chaos and ask myself what it is I needed at that moment, I realized that on one level I had expectations of myself to 'get a grip' and work things out. For instance, the children not listening to me and continuing to do their own thing and express themselves might be appropriate child-like behaviour when they are together. But at a deeper level, I had a need to be heard, to be accepted, validated, to have connection, to be safe, and to have peace.

3. **How did you get through those moments? What did you need to do within yourself to keep going? (I know you kept going because you are here reading these words at this moment in time.)**

For example: I needed to acknowledge to myself what was going on for me. I needed to get in touch with what I was really yearning for and then asked myself what I could do about that. How else could I meet my needs to be heard, to have peace, and to be safe? I slowed myself down by taking some deep breaths. I also needed to work on consciously being kind and compassionate towards myself instead of beating myself up with nasty self-talk. I then needed to look at some of the smaller steps that could be taken to walk through this to the other side and then took action, one step at a time, one moment at a time, and one breath at a time.

You gain **strength, courage, and confidence** by every experience in which you really stop to look **fear in the face**.

- Eleanor Roosevelt

3

Reacting to Chaos: Fear and Anger

When you are in a state of chaos, you experience some pretty intense, reactive emotions. Fear and anger are two states that most people try to avoid because both of these come from a sense of helplessness or lacking control. They also happen to be the primary reactions in chaos.

I used to think that Fear and Anger were not such great emotions to have — I mean, it certainly did not feel good to have that extreme visceral experience driving me to either run away and hide or pounce in a defensive attack. I worked very hard to avoid situations that would provoke these reactive experiences in order to avoid those feelings. Others may have had no clue that I was afraid of fear, especially if they knew that I used to sky-dive, bungee jump, and was always open to other adventurous, adrenaline-filled activities. But while those activities certainly had risks on a physical level, it was the emotional risks that I was afraid of — risks like sharing what was really going on for me inside, confrontations or any kind of conflict, or putting myself in situations where I had no control of what might happen. I think I had a fear of truly being seen because my fear told me "if I was truly seen for all that I am, surely I would not be liked." Gulp. My anger was not afraid to show up and express itself, though I certainly did not like how I felt when it was roaring through me, fighting for whatever it was wanting at that particular moment in time. My anger fought for me to be seen and heard, while my fear fought for me to hide and be invisible. No wonder there was chaos!

When the chaos became too overwhelming, Fear would eventually win over and I did what I knew how to do best when feeling stressed and overwhelmed: I avoided. I avoided sharing what was really going on for me (my experience), I avoided confrontation, I avoided any situation for which I could not fully predict the outcome, and I avoided allowing myself to be vulnerable and open with most of the people around me. I was that kid who faked being sick so I could stay home from school to avoid participating in a debate competition, not because I was afraid of the actual speech but because I was so afraid of the unpredictability of the rebuttal. I was also quite good at hiding this part of me so that most people, other than those who really knew me well, had no clue that I was so skillful at this avoidance tactic.

FACING THE FEAR

That turning point in my life when my husband was diagnosed with Stage 4 Non-Hodgkin's Lymphoma and given a prognosis of weeks to live confronted me in a way that nothing had, and prevented any possibility of avoidance. Chaos was definitely put into motion, engulfed in the tornado of the unknown and the fear that went along with it. There was no running away. There was no way to hide from the diagnosis and the potential of what it meant for our lives. Having to face the Fear and also acknowledge Anger was extremely overwhelming and I realized that all I could truly do was take one moment at a time, one breath at a time, and allow hope to carry me through each moment. That pivotal moment left me altered, requiring me to accept the journey of facing the situation and going through it no matter what the outcome. It also taught me to experience gratitude for each moment that we had with one another in the midst of the chaos of the unknown. The gift of the experience was the learning to be more deliberate and conscious about truly living in the absolute present moment. We can transform our fear and anger and do not need to be defined by the chaos.

TRANSFORMATION AND TRIUMPH

It was October 26, eight days after our daughter was born. Lufthansa flight number 492 from Frankfurt, Germany was landing at the Vancouver International Airport at exactly 11:10AM. What was so special about this particular flight? On board was a man whose job it was to transport stem cells from a donor's home country to the recipient wherever they might be in the world. This man had with him the very stem cells that were destined to reach my husband at Vancouver General Hospital. It was like an episode of one of those hospital dramas, only this was real life! On October 26, with a focused determination to live, Rod watched from his hospital room window on the 15th floor as the large 747 airplane flew over the mountains to land. It was an amazing moment for him: to allow it to sink in that this very aircraft was carrying the stem cells that later that same day were transferred straight from the airport to the hospital, up to the 15th floor, into his room and directly into Rod's Hickman line.

In Rod's own words:

I can recall the day of the stem cell transplant - October 26, 2007. What is odd is that I can actually recall it through the haze of all the hospital-grade drugs that were racing into my system through that Hickman funnel. I had been nuked with intense head-to-toe radiation therapy to knock out the weak remnants of my immune system, the better to avoid graft-versus-host disease, which mentally messed me up even more. But I do remember looking out my 15th floor window and seeing, way off in the distance, a Lufthansa plane making its way to YVR. We knew that the stem cell donor had been found in Germany somewhere, so maybe…?

Two hours later, the preserved stem cells were hanging on one of the multitude of IV lines. I think that the nurses on duty that day were a bit confused as to why there was no family around to see the cells being administered — apparently a common thing around the ward. But I didn't want it that way. It was a quiet, still and contemplative moment. Maybe a private moment.

As I reflect on this now, I still remember arriving back at the hospital and looking at the small, empty bag after its contents had been transferred directly into Rod. I sent up another prayer for these cells to work their magic, marvelling at how this medically perfect match could possibly be the catalyst that changed the original death sentence he had been given by the doctors at the beginning of this roller coaster ride. It was a moment of reprieve, yes, but it was also the beginning of what was perhaps one of the most challenging months of this journey as we waited to see if Rod's body would accept and embrace these foreign cells.

He was sick. He was exhausted. He was constantly monitored and confined to his hospital room. The intense and merciless treatments were no walk in the park. In fact, they were far from easy but I am convinced that strong will and determination were huge factors in Rod's healing journey. Acknowledging the fear and facing it without giving it any power or control. I believe that is what courage is. To quote Nelson Mandela: "I learned that courage was not the absence of fear, but the triumph over it."

For us, triumph over fear meant facing it every time it came up for either one of us. It meant not avoiding it or numbing out to the fear, and it also meant not giving into the fear or allowing it to be in charge. Triumph over fear is a process of acknowledgement, acceptance, and deciding how best to face it. Not allowing fear to be in charge. Rod knew what he had been dealt, and with every moment, he decided he would live.

POST - STEM CELL TRANSPLANT

Rod continued to defy all of his doctors' predictions and prognoses, even in the midst of his most challenging days — probably the most difficult of the whole process. His doctor had told him that he would likely be in the hospital for at least another six weeks as they administered anti-rejection drugs and monitored for graft-versus-host disease, which is what can happen sometimes when one's body decides to reject the transplant. Even then, Rod simply said, "Nope, I will be ready to go home in three weeks." The doctors knew by then not to argue with him, and this particular doctor smiled in a way that suggested support for Rod's hopes but with a disbelief that it would actually be a possibility for him to go home in three weeks.

My husband was sick in a way that was different from the chemotherapy symptoms. With the four rounds of intense chemotherapy he had been through, the phases of symptoms had almost become predictable which meant he had become somewhat prepared for what to expect. However, the full-body radiation treatment and stem cell transplant were brand new experiences, which meant he could not predict what would happen next, no matter how much research or information he had about it. Reading about it is not the same as experiencing it. About seven different medications were pumping through his Hickman line, each with their own effect and associated side-effects. The combination was unpredictable.

He was hooked up to a self-administering morphine dosage machine that was on a timer which allowed him to give himself a 'hit' when needed without overdosing. The first time Rod pushed the button to release a dose of this into his bloodstream, he felt a pretty intense rush that made him understand, in that instant, just how so many people get so intensely addicted to opioids. It scared him, and he decided to ration himself to two to three "hits" per day though he was allowed one dose every four hours as needed. It took some determination, and it was not the most comfortable of times, but he managed to get through that phase of major discomfort without becoming opioid-dependent.

Three weeks later, Rod's energy had increased, his blood counts were good, and he was itching to get out of the hospital. As he had predicted, despite what the doctors had said about him needing at least another six weeks in the hospital after the stem cell transplant, Rod was given the green light to come home. Yes, there was still more to get through before being completely in the clear and yes, there was still a year ahead of staying off work as he recovered from this ordeal, but for now we could celebrate the fact that he had defied all odds and was coming home to the adventures (and misadventures) of family and parenthood.

Ten years later, our adventures and misadventures continue without any signs of the cancer that was deemed incurable and terminal.

OPPORTUNITIES FOR GROWTH AND LEARNING

Each moment of every day has much to teach us if we are present and open to the opportunities for growth and learning. We can re-learn to just be, to come back to what is true in a moment in time rather than allowing pre-conceived notions to run wild in our imaginations. This is all part of the journey back to oneself — back to the essence of who we really are. My own journey back has been one of learning to trust that voice within my Self and having more courage to take risks. Daring more in all directions: emotional risks in sharing myself more, intellectual risks in speaking out my ideas even when they contradict what others are saying, and intuitive risks in acting on creative inspirations that turn into new interventions in therapy sessions with my clients. I do not have to allow Fear or Anger to be in charge of me. Rather, I can be more responsible in what I do with Fear and Anger when they appear.

I know that both Fear and Anger have such positive intentions for me and for my survival. The goal is *not* to become fearless or without anger because the truth is, both are needed for our basic survival. Fear is a necessary warning signal that lets us know when we are in danger. Anger gives us energy to assert ourselves when we need to be seen and heard. However, we don't need our fear or anger for matters of sharing our gifts and our Selves with the world. We do not need fear for creative expression. Fear still tends to show up anyway, causing us those butterflies and concerns and often appearing as what feels like a vulnerability hangover when we fear that maybe we have shared too much of ourselves with the world.

Now here is the truth about my relationship with Fear: when that particular stress comes to visit, I can still be very good at avoidance. It comes down to me making a decision to not let fear drive my actions. I consciously work on staying grounded and connected in spite of the fear. I can stay focused on what is true for each moment in time. Instead of using avoidance to run away from my feelings, I can make a deliberate decision to change my tendency of steering clear of situations that are uncomfortable to avoid being swallowed up and engulfed in the Fear. It is simply *being present* that helps me. It is very difficult to avoid something when it's right in front of you, so the present moment is where I choose to stay.

In transforming your own relationship with Fear, you can certainly allow Fear to come along for the ride but do not allow it to be in charge. Not unless it is actually the right time for Fear to be in charge, like if you are being chased by a tiger, in which case you might like to hand the wheel to Fear to direct your actions for survival purposes! When Fear does arise at inappropriate times for you, you can acknowledge it and then thank it for reminding you that you are alive and that you have a strong desire to fully live. You are here not to merely survive, where Fear dominates, but to thrive. We all have the capacity to thrive in this journey of human experience. The journey starts within — the journey home within your Self — then spreads between individuals, before continuing out among the rest of the world.

Virginia Satir sums it all up so beautifully: "Peace Within, Peace Between, Peace Among." When we can fully experience and embrace peace within ourselves, we can then have more peace and depth in our relationships with others leading to peace among all.

QUESTIONS FOR REFLECTION:

1. **How would you describe your relationship with Fear?**

   For example: how do you respond and react when fears come up for you? Do you avoid it? Face it head on? Fight it?

   I am aware of my fear when it shows up and acknowledge it for what it is. My fear serves to viscerally remind me of what is important to me: survival, living, my caring for the safety of those I love, and wanting to do a good job in whatever I do.

2. **How would you describe your relationship with Anger?**

For example: How do you respond and react when anger comes up for you? Are there differences between when it is your own anger that comes up and when it is others' anger that is being directed towards you or others? Do you stuff it down, explode, fight back, or keep it a secret?

I think I can be quite versatile in doing all of these things depending on who I am with, what the context is, and how grounded I am within myself at the time. When my own anger arises, it gives me a burst of energy that can either be helpful (like when I am standing up for myself or for somebody else) or it can be harmful (like when the anger gets too big and I say hurtful things or I let it eat away at me). When anger is directed at me from others, my response depends on how centred I am at that moment. Either I can accept their anger and be curious about the hurt or fear underneath it, or I can fall into my old pattern of wanting to keep the peace doing whatever it takes to calm the other person down.

3. **If you could have a dialogue with Fear and Anger, what would you want to tell them? What would you want them to know about how you want to be when they come up for you?**

For example: I would want Fear to know that I appreciate it for wanting to keep me safe. I can allow Fear to be there to warn me about any impending danger, but I also need to decipher whether the danger is real or not. I do not want Fear to be the one running the show because it gets in the way of my creativity and me undertaking risks to try new things.

I would want Anger to know that I appreciate it for speaking up about what I need that I may not be getting at that moment. I am grateful for Anger's intention of wanting justice and peace in my world and the world at large. I would like to listen to the messages of Anger when it comes up to allow me to make decisions about what I need in that moment in time. I would like Anger and Compassion to become more acquainted so that I can notice the anger, hear its message, and give compassion to myself and others which then allows the anger to transform.

3. **What are you deciding about how you would like to transform your relationship with Fear and Anger?**

   For example: With both Fear and Anger, I would like to be able to be more accepting of them when they come up rather than fighting them. I will listen to what is going on beneath the surface for the Fear or Anger, and to pay more attention to their yearnings. I would like to get back to a centred place more quickly, and from this place I know I would respond authentically from my heart and from my best intentions rather than from a reactive state of fear or anger

The **middle is messy**, but it's also where the **magic happens**.
- Brené Brown

4

Transforming our Relationship with the Past

It is not the moment itself that transforms, rather it is the alchemy of what happens in those moments that is transformational. It is the coming together of body, mind, heart, soul and spirit that creates something entirely new and different from what was before. The moment the egg and sperm come together to activate your life energy is transformational. The moment the butterfly emerges from the cocoon (and every moment leading up to that moment) is transformational. The moment you truly let go of the baggage of the past that you have been carrying throughout your life is transformational. The moment is sacred. The moment is inspired. These moments can happen spontaneously or they can be the result of moving through chaos, getting to the other side and knowing you are different for having gone through it.

TIME ZONES

The past is not the present. Yet here we are in the present, where we often find ourselves living out old patterns that were learned in the past. Your subconscious has no concept of time zones. When you dwell on memories from the past or worries about the future, your subconscious responds as though they are happening now, in the present. This can get messy and downright confusing as you try to figure out why you are reacting a certain way or why you suddenly want to burst out crying, or laughing out loud. It's as if part of you is functioning in a different time zone. Have you ever had the experience of walking along, out in public, when you think of a funny incident that happened yesterday or last year or a decade ago, and you laugh out loud? Your laughter has nothing to do with anything actually occurring in the immediate environment outside you and yet your physiological and behavioural responses are as though the funny incident had happened just now, here in the present. Or do you ever let your imagination run wild and think of worst case scenarios when your child does not come home when they were supposed to? If you allow your imagination to run with it you can really work yourself into a frenzy, again reacting in the present to something that has not actually happened. This lack of time zone in your subconscious can bring havoc and create barriers to truly being in the now. What can you do about that? The task becomes separating what is the past, the present and the future. How can you put all that baggage you have been carrying back into the past where it actually belongs? You don't need to take it with you on your journey. It is possible that maybe you didn't even realize that.

Your Baggage

Your baggage can take on many forms — secrets are big ones. Secrets, when they remain hidden, end up festering and rotting away at your insides. Feelings of anger, resentment, shame and guilt take their toll on your physical, mental, emotional, and spiritual health. Carrying secrets blocks your flow of energy, diminishing your capacity to fully embrace and live Life.

To create more space and freedom within, you will need to unhook yourself from any impacts from the past that may have continued to have a hold on you and your life. This is your time to embrace Life. There is no need to be held back, to hide in corners or to be invisible.

You learned how to survive in this world, in your culture, and in the family (or families) where you grew up. Survival is a good thing, however, some of what you learned about surviving can actually be getting in your way of thriving and embracing life fully. Not all traits that served you then are helping you now.

KEEPING IT ALL INSIDE: "JOE"

"Joe" was referred to me when he was released from the psychiatric unit after having had a 'breakdown' and severe panic attacks. He wanted to work on resolving his anxiety as it was getting in the way of his everyday life. After exploring how his anxiety shows up and what triggers it, we began to get to the root of when his anxiety first arose. He mentioned, in passing, that his mother had died when he was nine and he then continued to talk about something else. I stopped him, returning to his memory of his mother dying. He said he had been close with her and when she died he was sent to school the very next day. She was never talked about again. He had not been allowed to process his grief and sadness over losing his mother. His father had never talked about it, his brother had never talked about it, and his extended family had never talked about it. It was as if the existence of his mother and her death had never occurred. Therein was the root of a subconscious decision he had made to 'keep it all inside' and 'never talk about my emotional pain.' We know that emotions and memory are stored at a cellular level in the body. When these are not released and processed, whether by circumstance or choice, they show themselves somehow and eventually our bodies let us know. We explode in anger, we have a panic attack, or we break down.

The therapy sessions with Joe became about processing his grief, allowing him to experience and express the pain of losing his mother. Experiencing the pain of the loss did not feel good for him but having his pain and his experience witnessed and held with acceptance and love allowed him to move through it. His panic attacks have stopped. He is showing up more fully for his life now and feeling more at ease. He is even opening up conversation with family members to start talking about his mom again.

WHEN THE PAST IMPACTS THE PRESENT

When my daughter was four years old, we were hiking on some lovely trails in the forest when a large dog (which must have seemed like a giant to my daughter) came bounding up to her and knocked her off the trail. She was terrified, and thus began her fear of dogs. This has impacted her enjoyment of hiking in the woods for fear of encountering an off-leash dog. Several years later, she still struggles being around dogs. She still startles when she sees a dog on the trail and her flight response is on full steam as she runs to hold onto me. Her fear is initially at the forefront. Her past continues to impact her in the present and blocks her from being able to fully enjoy the now when in a situation where she might encounter a dog.

If we look at the positive intention of her avoidance, we know that her avoidance serves to prevent another incident of being startled and knocked over by a dog. But we can also look at the cost of her avoidance. That fear response grips her body and disconnects her from her joy. As Jean-Paul Sartre said, "What is important is not what happens to us but how we respond to what happens to us." It is not about the dog knocking her over. It is about the startle response, the emotions that she had, the meaning she made, and whatever subconscious decision was made in that moment regarding what she needed to do to survive with dogs. Her fear comes from what she did with the impact of the event. We continue to work on new ways of responding when we encounter dogs on the trails to help support her in knowing that it is a different situation with a different potential outcome. This is a work in progress! Some days are better than others, and it is important to know that not all change happens overnight.

YOU CAN CHANGE THE IMPACT THE PAST HAS TODAY

Your past can truly block you from fully living. The good news is that, while you can't change the past, you can change the impacts from the past. Because you are the one who created the impact by whatever it was that you did, you are therefore also the one who can change the impact. Isn't that wonderful to know? When you allow yourself to reflect on how you have been impacted and become aware of what you have been carrying with you that is not really needed for the present, you can be more in charge of the choices for what you want to do. The impact of a previous situation doesn't need to determine the impact of a current one. You can decide what it is that you want to change even when you are not entirely sure about how you will change it. Knowing the 'what' is an important part. Sometimes you need some help with the 'how' and sometimes the 'how' will reveal itself to you. Often, you might realize that you have been holding onto hurt, anger, resentment, shame and guilt from the past that you really do not need to carry forward in your life anymore. These emotional impacts may have become a part of your status quo without your conscious awareness. These old hurts and fears, old triggers and old wounds, are of no help to you in contributing to living a more vibrant life. Showing up for life more fully means letting go and transforming the impacts from the past.

Letting Go Versus Giving Up

People sometimes confuse the difference between letting go and giving up. When we give up, there remains a residual feeling of loss that may include sadness, powerlessness and somehow, a sense of giving up on yourself. Letting go involves empowerment of our selves and may need a process of healing. When you give up, you are still holding on. When you let go, you are free. You can bring the learnings of the experience with you, as there are lessons and wisdom to be gained from what happens in your life. You can carry the wisdom forward as you welcome and greet new opportunities in the present. You let go by moving through rather than avoiding, ignoring, and distorting what happened. By recognizing and moving through a situation, you allow the current of your emotions, thoughts, expectations, and your yearnings to flow through to the letting go.

When it is difficult to let go, ask yourself: "What is it that I still want that I am not getting?" Sometimes what is wanted may not be very useful, such as revenge or getting even; holding onto anger because it fuels something. But what is going on underneath the revenge and anger? If you look deep enough you will find hurt, pain, sadness, disappointment and, maybe even fear.

I had a client who wanted her mother to tell her she loved her and to give her more physical affection, yet her mother had died several years earlier. Helping my client to identify what it was that she wanted led to working on accepting that she would not be able to receive that in the present, and to believe that if her mother had known how to do things differently she would have. We then explored the areas in her life where she was currently receiving love and physical affection. Helping her to love herself more and to appreciate her mother for doing the best that she knew how allowed my client to let go of the pain associated with her unmet wants.

What we are wanting may not always be logical, but the emotions are real. Our past has an impact on our present. The unexpressed and unidentified emotions that get stored in our body, the thoughts and decisions that get made consciously or unconsciously, the way others have responded or reacted to us and our responses and reactions to others: all of it impacts us in the now. As Virginia Satir eloquently stated, we cannot change the past but we can change the impacts of the past. The problem really is not the problem. It's in the way that we cope and react that creates the problem for us. We can actually resolve our past, let it go and transform the impacts so we can be more free to fully live in the present. To truly let go of the baggage from our past, we need to allow ourselves to be with the chaos that might get stirred up. Within the chaos there exists an infinite number of new possibilities that can come into our awareness when we allow ourselves to stay in it rather than returning to our former status quo.

CHANGING FROM THE INSIDE OUT

When you have a genuine transformational shift, everything changes from the inside out. It truly is transformational change at a cellular level. Imagine the butterfly and its ultimate transformation — dramatically changing in physical form. Imagine what that first experience of unfurling wings might have been like for the one-time caterpillar: moving from merely crawling and exploring what is close to the earth, the details of the leaf, the climbing of a stem to a whole new world of flight, new heights, new soaring, new experience and new possibilities. That is what transformational change is all about — seeing the world from a whole new perspective, unfurling our wings, and soaring in the glorious freedom of flight with the breeze, the winds, and the new challenges that come along with new experience.

The experiential process of letting go, forgiving yourself and others, and truly connecting with your joy and freedom will lead to changes in every part of you. Your feelings transform, old beliefs about you are no longer valid and new beliefs take their place. Every cell in your body resonates with the impact of transformational change. The way you relate with yourself and others changes. People even look different when they have shifted their whole experience of themselves and others; their eyes have more sparkle to them, their faces have more colour, and their vitality shows in their energy and their physical presence. A transformational change is so much more profound than merely changing behaviours. It is in those a-ha moments that the magical alchemy of new awareness and insights arise, allowing new experiences within your innermost Self.

When we **feel good** mentally, emotionally, and physically, we naturally **generate more energy** and hope.
- Jennifer Nagel

5

A Case Example of Transformational Change: 'Jack'

I remember the first time I met Jack. Any sense of joie de vivre was completely absent and I had a feeling that Jack had been disconnected from his experience of joy for quite some time. He had been diagnosed with depression, and his doctor was recommending that he go for therapy. Jack had a great deal of anxiety and worry about his inability to provide for his family. He was off work on disability due to his chronic and debilitating depression. He was anxious about the unknowns of the future and the impacts of all of this on his wife and young child.

Jack shared the difficulties he was having in every moment of his day and how challenging it was just to motivate himself to get going. Sleep was his place of refuge and escape. To get out of bed in the morning was a huge feat for him, but then the idea of facing the day and doing anything productive was overwhelming. He was stuck and not feeling very hopeful.

Yet here he was in my office with his wife who came to support him in that first visit.

"Tell me about the part of you that got you here to my office. The part of you that wants something different for your life?" I asked him. I wanted to connect with the part of him that held onto hope that things could be different. I wanted Jack to connect with that part so he could start to awaken to the more positive energy that hope brings along with it.

We explored what he hoped to have different in his life and he shared his desire to experience more joy, to be able to be more fully present in the moment, and to be healthy. Beautiful!

"Can you imagine what that would look like — to have more joy? What would be different for you?"

"How else would you feel?"

"How would you experience your wife and child differently?"

These were some of the questions that guided Jack to creating a picture of what it would look like for him to have more joy.

"What happens inside (your body) as you are in touch with how you would like to be?"

Jack noticed the juxtaposition of his experience of the pain and sadness around his depression, and his experience of hope for how he would like to be. This new energy of hope felt good to Jack, but he wasn't certain how he would get there.

"What gets in the way of you experiencing more joy?"

Thus began our exploration of how Jack experienced his depression and the painful cost in all areas of his life. As we explored, Jack really connected with his sadness around the depression. I asked him where in his body did he experience his sadness the most. Jack brought his hands to his core. I invited him to close his eyes and go there, to put his attention there. Jack did this willingly and his breathing slowed as he allowed himself to connect with this part of him.

"How big is it?...Does it have a shape?...A colour?"

Jack described it as a large, grey blob. We got to know this grey blob and asked it some questions such as what did it want for Jack's life? What was it protecting him from? We even sent this grey blob, the depression, some appreciation for the intentions it had of keeping him safe even if the way in which it was trying to keep him safe was not very helpful due to it getting in the way of Jack fully living and enjoying his life.

After some time of really experiencing this grey blob of sadness and getting to know the depression and its positive intentions better, I asked Jack, "If you could change the colour, what colour would you like it to be?"

Without hesitation, Jack responded that he would like it to be blue. I invited him to imagine breathing blue into this area. He had already sent some appreciation to it and now we were adding the colour blue. Jack's body visibly relaxed as he did this. A smile came to his face as he experienced the different energy that the blue brought with it. Jack was starting to learn ways to be more in charge of his emotions rather than having his emotions be in charge of him. This felt good to him and added some more energy to his hope. He had more positive feelings about himself which were being experienced physiologically in his body, and expressed through more positive language which reflected a shift in his thoughts and beliefs about himself. When we feel good mentally, emotionally, and physically, we naturally generate more energy and hope.

SESSION 2

The next time I met with Jack, he was feeling very anxious again and complained of racing thoughts and being unable to focus on the present. He was in touch with feelings of guilt, shame, sadness and fear. In other words, he was experiencing chaos. First we worked on getting grounded. Breathing, guided visualization, and reconnecting with the present. That meant getting connected with whatever was happening at *this* very moment in time: focusing only on what was true for that particular moment in time and not focusing on all of the what-ifs and the catastrophic thinking about a future that was not even real at that moment.

We worked on noticing the feelings without judgment.

We worked on noticing the thoughts without judgment.

As feelings and thoughts came up for Jack, he visualized them as clouds floating by; Noticing them and accepting them. He realized that fighting the feelings and thoughts only made them bigger and stronger. Accepting them meant allowing them to be there but not fixating on them or holding onto them. He also became aware that if he did not judge his feelings and simply allowed them to be there, they automatically started to shift and change on their own.

We then worked on adding more supportive thoughts to the unsupportive thoughts. For example: "I am not good enough" (unsupportive thought) was replaced with "I am enough and I am on my journey of growth" (supportive thought). We also continued working on imagining the future and how he wanted it to be rather than how he feared it could be. By connecting with the imagined future, the body can experience this physiologically in the present as if it were already happening now. His homework after that session was to practice spending time focusing on his breath, noticing thoughts and feelings without judgment, and replacing unsupportive thoughts with supportive ones.

SESSION 3

By the third session a huge shift had already taken place. Jack had been spending a few minutes each day visualizing his imagined Self of who he wanted to be in relationship with himself, his family, and others in his life. He entered the office in much brighter spirits than I had ever experienced him before this moment. Jack announced that his mood had lifted and he was feeling more hopeful than he had in a long time. We explored what he was doing within himself to help support this change.

The work of this session became a couples session between Jack and the Depression. We worked to form a new relationship with depression by fully separating the two members of the couple: 'Jack' and 'the depression'. Rather than taking the statement, "I am depressed" as a truth, I asked Jack this question:

"Who is the 'I' that feels depressed?"

In this exploration, we were untangling and de-enmeshing the "I" — that core essence of who Jack was and is underneath the depression — from the Depression. Jack concluded that Truth is the "I" and he believed that Depression had been trying to disconnect him from that. It turns out that the Depression actually wanted the same things for Jack's life that Jack did: love, acceptance, belonging, to be significant and seen. When Jack realized that he and Depression really did want the same things but that Depression was going about trying to help him in a way that really was not all that helpful, he visibly relaxed his body and also sat up a little straighter with a huge smile on his face. Thus began a new conversation and relationship with Depression.

Jack decided that if and when Depression decided to visit him, he would "have tea" with Depression and say "Thank you for the reminder of what I want in my life. I am on my journey." And then after acknowledging and accepting Depression and appreciating its positive intentions, he would send it on its way.

Later in that very same session, Jack was given an opportunity to actually practice this when his sadness suddenly came up again. It really was a gift to witness him actually go through the process of recognizing the sadness, accepting it, appreciating it, and stating his truth about being on his journey. Jack experienced immediate relief and lightness as he also started giving more attention to happiness and joy.

SESSION 4

Jack arrived at his next appointment continuing to experience more hope and more happiness. He told me he was more positive, more present, and experiencing more purpose in his day. He was even getting out to look for opportunities to start volunteering as well as checking out community centre classes that he was interested in taking for recreation!

Again, we reviewed what he was doing inside as I really wanted him to own that he was the one doing the work to not only sustain the shifts he had already made, but to continue growing and enhancing himself from these shifts. Jack was truly showing signs of being more present for his life, and his wife and child were also reaping the benefits of these changes. As his relationship with himself transformed, so did his relationships with the people in his life.

In this session we did an exercise where I had Jack draw several circles on a piece of paper. Each circle represented some aspect of his life, including himself, family members, hobbies and interests. I invited him to write words or draw images inside the circles of qualities and adjectives to describe what he liked and appreciated about each one. For example, for himself he wrote the words "caring, kind, and loyal." After all these circles were filled, I had him connect with what had been getting in his way and write words to represent the unsupportive thoughts outside of the circles. He wrote things like "I am a failure. I am not good enough. I will never succeed." Having this visual representation where the essence of his true self was inside the circles, and the old beliefs that were not doing him any favours were outside of the circles really helped him to see these unsupportive thoughts as "noise" getting in his way. The noise that was interfering with his connection with who he really was and is at his core.

We spent time emphasizing and anchoring into this new awareness and how this impacted his experience of himself; what had changed in his feelings, his beliefs, his expectations, and his deeper yearnings for acceptance, connection and peace.

SESSION 5

We took a longer break in between sessions to see how these shifts and changes would impact him in his life. When I saw him next, Jack proudly reported that his doctor told him he was ready to ease back into work again as he had made significant improvements and no longer fit the criteria to be off work on disability. He also told me that he had booked a family trip overseas for the holidays. This was huge! Not only was he imagining how he wanted things to be, but he also was taking action to make it happen! Jack was continuing to use the mindfulness strategies we had worked on and was making time to process his experience through journaling each day. We celebrated the changes that Jack had made and spent time appreciating the journey. Re-visiting where he had been when he first started coming for therapy brought up feelings of sadness for him when he remembered how helpless he had felt. Experiencing the sadness of where he had been also allowed him to fully experience his gratitude for getting through it to the other side. We mutually agreed that no more counselling appointments were needed. Jack had all the resources he needed within himself to continue on his journey.

It's important to remember that we all have **magic inside us**.
 - JK Rowling

6

Connecting With Your Life Energy

Your life energy can flow with more ease when you remove the old blocks and triggers that get in your way. You don't need to have your energy drained by the old stuff you tend to carry around. Here is the good news that may not sound that good at first. The blocks and triggers belong to you. They are yours. You created them by how you internalized and processed your experiences. Now, you are probably wondering what exactly could be so good about that. Because the blocks and triggers are yours and you created them, you can actually do something about that. You can change them! It's true, you may need some help along the way but change is truly possible and it is yours to decide what you would like to do about that.

You can do more than merely adjust to your circumstances, or adjust to another person's way of being. You can connect with your resources of love, acceptance and caring which then allow you to connect more deeply with yourself and others. When you do this, you are showing up more authentically for your life. You may not even realize right now that you have choice in how you show up, when you show up, and whether you show up for your life. The essence of who you are is just waiting for you to reconnect and become fully present. Life energy — your life energy — is what keeps you moving towards growth and change. It is also what allows your body to do the work of healing when it is injured, and what allows for change and transformation to take place physically, emotionally, mentally and spiritually. Every single one of us that is alive and breathing has life energy.

HOW DOES LIFE ENERGY GET EXPERIENCED?

Trying to explain what it is like to experience life energy is similar to trying to explain what it is like to taste chocolate. No matter how many descriptive words you might find to explain what chocolate tastes like, there is nothing in any vocabulary that will truly do justice to depicting this experience. The only way to truly know about chocolate is to taste it. But let me do my best attempt for you to taste or experience what I mean when I am referring to life energy.

If you can, I would like you to find a place to be right now where there are no distractions or extra noise to interfere with the following, brief exploration.

Now sit or stand in a way that you are physically comfortable and relaxed, and allow the following visualization to guide you. If this is too challenging to do through reading, you could also record yourself reading it and then listen to your own voice guiding you or ask someone else to read it to you:

Allow your body to relax and begin to just notice your breathing. Allow your breath to be deep and see if you can follow your breath in through your nose, down into your lungs, and out into your bloodstream, bringing oxygen to every cell in your body. Just be aware of your body and invite each part to relax.

Next, imagine a time or place when you felt really good about being you, even if it was for only a moment. Really allow yourself to get in touch with this experience when you may have felt full of peace, joy, harmony, and love. Maybe you felt a deep connection with everyone and everything. Think of times where you have this experience: maybe when out in nature, or listening to beautiful music, or a moment with someone you love. Just close your eyes for a moment and allow yourself to really get in touch with what that experience was like.

Now, imagine that you have a spark of light inside of you and allow yourself to connect with that light. Allow it to grow a little and breathe into it… and allow it to grow even more until light fills your whole body… going down your legs through the tips of your toes… going down your shoulders and arms through to your fingertips… going up your neck, head and face..Imagine your whole body being filled with light and notice what that experience feels like. Make that light as bright as you want it to be.

Now let that light grow even bigger so that it goes outside your body and around your body, enveloping you in light. Notice what is happening in your body. You may feel some sensations, tingling, heat, cold, or nothing at all. Know that whatever you are experiencing is OK.

Notice how you are feeling right now and how you are experiencing yourself. In this place of connection with your light, imagine someone you care about coming to stand in front of you and they bring with them their own light. How is it for you to imagine your essence and their essence meeting each other? How does that person seem to you at this moment as you imagine him or her? Allow yourself to imagine having a dialogue with this person from this place of connection. Allow yourself to send love and caring to this person, and also allow yourself to receive their love and caring.

Whether or not you have this kind of connection in reality, know that you can hold this connection in your heart — that it can be possible to meet others, essence to essence.

Again, notice your life energy around you and inside of you and know that you can connect here more consciously in your life. You can take moments to breathe, connect with your light, and experience yourself fully.

Breathe this all in right now, taking in what you need for you... and breathe out whatever you no longer need to carry, creating more space for authentic connection within yourself and in relationship with others.

Take a moment now to reflect on whatever you just experienced. Journal about it too if you are so inclined.

HOW DO WE RE-CONNECT AFTER BEING TRIGGERED?

The essence of who we are is always there for us to connect with and fully experience, but we are not always connected at this place. We get triggered. We get blocked. Experiences happen in our lives that have an impact on how we see ourselves, others and the world around us. Experiences happen that we make decisions about how to keep ourselves safe whether physically, emotionally, or spiritually, in order for us to survive. The flow of our life energy can get blocked. The good news is that it does not need to remain blocked. We can transform, change, and remove the blocks to restore flow and connection. We can re-connect and return to who we truly are at our essence. We are born whole and we continue to be whole. We sometimes forget that and see ourselves as broken.

When you recognize that you have been triggered, take a moment to pause. Breathe in deeply to slow down the internal chaos, and allow yourself to acknowledge and accept that you were triggered. You can be curious about it, but if you are needing to re-connect more immediately in the present, you can put whatever it was that triggered you "on the shelf" with a commitment to look at it and resolve it later. You can then go through the meditation of connecting with your light, reminding yourself and your body of the experience of connection with your life energy. Or you can find whatever ritual fits for you to consciously reconnect and ground yourself. Practice this ritual daily, triggers or no triggers, as the more you practice the more automatic it will become to reconnect with your life energy when needed.

EXERCISE TO CONNECT WITH YOUR INNER RESOURCES

1. Write down the words "I am…" and complete the phrase. For example: "I am compassionate." Continue writing sentences beginning with "I am…" and allow your list to grow, with room to add more as it comes to you.

2. Think about what other resources are involved with each of the qualities you have listed so far and add to your list. For example: What are some of the other qualities I have that help me to be compassionate? Caring, empathic, loving. You can then add "I am caring, I am empathic, I am loving," to your list.

3. If you happen to list your various roles such as "I am a spouse. I am a friend. I am a parent. I am a (whatever your profession is)", allow yourself to explore what qualities you bring to the many roles that you have. Do not be hard on yourself if you are thinking, "But I am not always patient or loving." The fact is that we are all human and if you are patient and loving sometimes then you still have these abilities, even if you are not always using them.

   For example: In my role of 'Mom' I bring qualities of playfulness, patience, loving, caring, and trustworthiness. I would add these to my list as: I am playful. I am patient. I am loving. I am caring. I am trustworthy. Now, I want to emphasize that I am not always playful and I am most certainly not always patient, but I do have these resources and qualities that get used in my role of 'Mom' sometimes. I want you to also list those qualities that you do hold, even if they don't always seem present.

4. Really give yourself time to sit with this exercise and go deep into your exploration of who you are.

5. Now read your list out loud, beginning each sentence with "I am…" Notice what happens in your energy as you say these words out loud.

Keep this list so that you can remind yourself of who you are at your core, as we all need reminders from time to time.

EXERCISE FOR IDENTIFYING THE BLOCKS

1. **Draw a large circle in the middle of the next page. Inside the circle, write down all the words from your "I am" list in the previous exercise.**

2. **Ask yourself what gets in the way of connecting with who you really are (the qualities inside the circle). What are some of the unsupportive thoughts and beliefs you have that can interfere sometimes? Write these down outside the circle.**

   For example: Thoughts such as "I am not good enough. I am unlovable. I cannot do this." Maybe you can also identify some triggers such as arguing with loved ones, feeling lonely, or not being heard. Maybe you can also identify some past experiences of abandonment or loss that are also interfering with being fully open to connection.

3. **Everything that is outside of the circle represents blocks to connection. Note that none of it actually gets inside of the circle and who you are at your core does not change. As you look at these blocks now, what "time zone" is each one in - is it a block from the past, present, or future?**

    For example:

    Past – a mistrust of people may come from past experiences of betrayal or abandonment.

    Present – some of my present perceptions of myself such as a belief that I do not have the ability to do something might be getting in my own way of moving forward.

    Future – Fears and worries about failure, worries about what could happen as opposed to what is happening.

4. **For each unsupportive thought or belief, write down what you would like to replace it with.**

    For example: "I am not good enough" (unsupportive belief) could be replaced with "I am enough" (supportive belief). "It is easier to stay quiet and be invisible" (unsupportive) might be replaced with "I have something to say and I deserve to be seen and heard" (supportive).

5. **What are you aware of wanting to change or let go of so that you can more easily stay in harmony with yourself?**

   For example: I want to change my self-deprecating thoughts to be more supportive and compassionate towards myself when I make mistakes, holding onto my desire and intention to do good work in the world and being alright with my imperfections while striving for continuous growth and learning.

Being fully present makes all the difference between **living in black and white** or **living in full technicolour**, full-sensory, surround-sound.
- Jennifer Nagel

7

Showing Up

Who were you before you sorted out and formed your identity? Who were you when you were first born, fresh into this world with new experiences at every moment? Who were you before you learned how to navigate relationships and be safe? You were certainly innocent and resourceful with all kinds of innate abilities the moment you emerged from the womb. For example, you knew how to take in that first breath of air and you knew exactly where to go for nourishment. You were born ready and open to be loved, accepted and cared for — ready for growth. No matter what life experiences you have been through and no matter how old you are, you never lose this readiness, this desire for love, acceptance and growth. In the very beginning, you naturally and instinctively showed up. You were so very present in the moment — knowing when you were hungry, when you wanted to be held, when you wanted to sleep, when you were experiencing discomfort or pain, and when you experienced nurturing. You could simply be exactly who you were and exactly where you were at exactly each moment in time. You were born ready to show up! No matter what you may have experienced in life since your birth, this readiness to show up remains. It is still there. Maybe now is the time to become more connected with this innate readiness. Maybe now is the time to wake up, to be more fully present and show up to fully live your life.

WHAT DOES IT MEAN TO SHOW UP?

Imagine if all you needed to do to live a successful and vibrant life was to simply show up. This means to actually be there, to be where you are at a moment in time and to fully embrace the present moment while being open to whatever presents itself to you. It also means to be in your full experience — to have more awareness, at every moment in time, of what is happening for you in your physical presence, your emotional world, your perceptions and thoughts, and your connection or disconnection from the freedom to be exactly who you are.

CASE STUDY: KRISTA

Krista had come for therapy because she wanted to be more secure and grounded in herself and wanted to feel less needy in relationships. She didn't want to define her worth by whether or not she was involved romantically with somebody else.

What was obstructing her path of fully showing up for her life in the present was left-over impacts from past relationships that she described as toxic and abusive. Shame and self-doubt had their ways of creeping into her relationships with others, and this was sabotaging any opportunity for new ways of being in relationship with herself and with others.

In our sessions together, Krista worked on being fully present to experience what was happening for her. She learned to separate out the negative self-talk and also to listen to what her body was saying to her. For example, she identified an area in her chest that wanted her to be free while also connecting with an area of tension in her sternum that wanted her to forgive herself and the family member who had abused her. Listening to her body's messages rather than denying them started paving the way for her to be more in the present and to be more honouring of herself.

As Krista cultivated more love and acceptance of herself, she also got in touch with a very deep yearning for more authentic connection with others. She became aware of how her protectiveness and need for control and safety had been distancing herself from others. She compared herself to a conductor: orchestrating how her interactions and connections with others went so that she could have the illusion of being in charge. We looked at the very positive intentions of this role of conductor as well as the cost to her. In her growing love and acceptance of herself, she could allow her own wisdom to determine whom she opens her heart to and whom she chooses not to be around.

Krista learned to honour all of her emotions, allowing them to just be there when they presented themselves to her. She learned to listen to her wisdom in the present, and to shift the internal voice that had been so very negative up until our work together. The voice of 'No' became the voice of 'Know.' Knowing what is true in the present moment and not confusing it with the past allowed Krista to re-awaken her innate ability to show up for her life.

OUR CAPACITY TO SHOW UP

The answer of being more present to all of your experience may sound simple but it certainly is not easy. As I have already stated, you were born ready to show up for your life with the capacity to experience a full range of emotions. You may have screamed and yelled in anger, cried in disappointment, laughed with joy, and giggled with silliness. Your body naturally and freely expressed your immediate emotions when you were very young, but you did not remain in this newborn state for long. This state changed as you began to navigate the complexities of the social environment (your family) in which you were raised. You learned in your family about what feelings and behaviours were acceptable and which were not. "Don't be sad." "There is no need to cry." "Don't get angry." "Stop that silliness." Maybe you began to hold things in as you figured out what was okay or not okay to express.

The fact is that all emotions are necessary. Having and experiencing the full range of emotions is part of fully experiencing Life. How can you truly know Joy if you also do not truly know Despair? Sure, you might experience surface level joy if you are repressing the other emotions, but to truly know the depths of Joy you need to be open to the other emotional experiences. The comparison is useful. When you stuff your emotions, they do not disappear but are stored at a cellular level in your body and may come out as physical discomfort, pain, or even illness. Emotions are neither good nor bad, but we learn to judge them as such and the way in which we judge them or repress them have all kinds of consequences for our mental, physical, emotional, and spiritual heath.

The Messages of Our Emotions

What if you were to see every emotion as having some kind of message for you with a positive intention? Perhaps your anger tells you that there is some kind of injustice that has happened. It might be reminding you that you deserve to be heard, to be seen, to belong, to connect and to love. Maybe your sadness is about disappointment or letting go; a loss of something. Your joy could be about the thrill of connection, love, belonging, and your engagement with Life. The list goes on. Every emotion, when permitted to just be experienced, allows you to better identify your deepest truth to enable you to fully live and show up for your Life.

Going Through the Muck

Showing up, being in the present moment and embracing the full experience does not always feel good. This is not about having life be all rainbows, butterflies and unicorns. This is about keeping it real and going through the goo, the muck, the stickiness, the messiness, the trials and tribulations, the joys and triumphs, the vulnerable tender moments, and the bold, courageous ones.

Betrayals, violations, jealousies, losses, fears, and hurts are not things we exactly wish to experience or desire to pursue. "The pursuit of betrayal" does not really have the same ring to it as "the pursuit of happiness." The muck of life is real and we can truly get stuck in it. How we face it, how we react or respond to it all, makes a huge difference in how we ultimately experience ourselves. The same is true in reverse; how we experience ourselves makes a huge difference in how we react or respond to it all.

SYSTEMIC NATURE

There is nothing linear about life whatsoever. It is all systemic, meaning that each and every part has an impact and influence on each and every other part. The thing about systems is when just one part of the system changes, the entire rest of the system changes too. It simply has to change because one slight shift impacts the whole balance of how the system had been working up until that point, whether it was dysfunctional or functional. Think of wind chimes or a mobile hanging over a baby crib. When one part of the mobile moves, the rest of the pieces in the mobile move too. What this means is that when one person in a couple or a family makes a shift or change in how they react and respond, or when a person makes a shift in how they experience themselves, this will in turn impact the reactions and responses of those with whom they are in contact. For better or for worse, it all changes.

When a parent starts responding to a child's attachment needs and yearnings for connection, belonging, love and significance rather than reacting to the behaviour, the child's behaviour will change because the way in which they experience themselves in your presence will change. I have experienced this first-hand with my own children. There are times when I react in anger to their fighting with one another, which generally tends to escalate the conflict. However, there are other times when I respond to what is going on underneath the fighting, such as acknowledging and validating my son's yearning for connection with his sister through play while she is yearning for independence through time alone. His hurt at her refusal to play with him shows up as yelling and threatening in his behaviour, but when I can acknowledge and validate both of their needs, the conflict de-escalates. When I change how I respond, they change in their responses also.

REACTING TO STRESS

We all have our ways of reacting when we are experiencing stress in our lives. Some people get really angry and find fault with everyone and everything else around them. Some people get really hurt and spend their energy trying to please everyone around them in order to feel accepted and liked. Some people are cut off from their emotions and seem almost robotic-like in their logical, linear, head-based response. Some people get so overwhelmed and over-loaded by their stress that they either react in a way that is completely irrelevant to what is going on around them (like cracking a joke, changing the subject, leaving the room) or they shut down and freeze. We all learn these ways of protecting ourselves and then we use them only when we are experiencing stress. Virginia Satir called these the Survival Coping

Stances and identified four main ways that are used: Blaming, Placating, Super-Reasonable, and Irrelevant. They are how we learned to survive in the families where we grew up.

Each member of the family learns their own way of surviving under stress. You can imagine the many different combinations of what this could look like. Under stress, one person might tend to blame someone else in the family while another person sacrifices their own needs for the sake of keeping the peace. Another family member might tend to avoid being around at all when there is tension and might stay at the office late or retreat to their room. Another family member might crack some jokes to ease the tension, or they might tend to have logical explanations for what is happening with little regard to how others are feeling. The way that others react under stress can perpetuate the dynamics of our own stress.

It is important to remember that we only do this under stress. If we are not experiencing stress, there is no need to be in our coping stances. We can be free to connect with who we truly are underneath all the roles and the façades and our behaviours.

GETTING OUT OF MY OWN WAY

I remember the first program I ever taught for therapists and other helping professionals in a foreign country. I was new to the culture and new to teaching in translation. That alone was enough to create some stress within me, and the first day was utter chaos. The temperature outside was sweltering hot and the air conditioning in the room was not working, creating discomfort and stress for the participants. We were forced to find another space after it became pretty clear that we would not function well in the heat. In the new room we moved to the microphone system was not working. Then we were faced with rather loud and intrusive construction noise outside, and once again we needed to find a new space. My survival coping pattern under stress tends to be placating and blaming. There was a part of me that placated throughout the day, wanting everyone to be okay and going along with the multitude of room changes. Another part of me was blaming and feeling frustrated and angry with what was going on, especially being the first day of a program when it is so imperative to build safety and connection within the group. The multitude of disruptions was getting in the way of any kind of smooth-flowing process. After I (barely) made it through the first day of the program the chaos and anxiety within me was quite huge and I still had five more days to go! A part of me wanted to run away, hop on the next flight home and give up on training overseas altogether. I was overwhelmed, exhausted, and had some nasty self-talk voicing itself inside my head. I also knew that I did not really have a choice about completing the program as there was no back-up trainer to take my place.

I woke early the next morning to meditate and went for a long walk up a mountain. It felt fantastic to get to the top and the view was spectacular. While I was taking in this view, a sudden peace came over me before I heard a voice so clearly from within saying, "Jennifer, just get out of your own way!" Of course! I had been getting in the way by allowing my stress and coping stance to use up a lot of my energy. I was the one creating my own stress by what I was telling myself about my abilities (or lack thereof) to do this work.

That was a total wake-up for me! I remember laughing out loud, alone there on that mountain. Of course! I was the one getting in my way! This had nothing to do with the air conditioning or the construction work or the room changes. I was the one blocking myself by getting caught up in my own stress and expectations about how it was all supposed to be. From that point on I made a decision to do my part by showing up, letting go of those persistent expectations of mine in order to be fully present for the bigger picture of the work I was here to do with this group. I had been showing up mentally and physically but had been hanging tightly to my own expectations and beliefs about how I believed the program should transpire. By "getting out of my own way" and deciding to be present for all of it, the rest of the program then flowed beautifully. I felt free, my intuition was on fire and the creativity within the program was abundant. The group was able to use their initial experience of chaos from the first part of the program as part of their own learning and growth around their response to chaos. The new container of safety allowed for deeper sharing and a willingness to do their own personal work so that they could more fully show up in their workplaces, in their families, and in their lives.

Had I been more fully present with myself and the group on that initial day of the program, my internal response to what was happening around us would have been very different. I imagine I would have been more open and accepting of the circumstances as they were completely out of my control. Rather than working so hard at trying to follow the curriculum outline — my expectation of what was meant to happen — I would have been more immediate in helping the group to process their experience of the external chaos and to use it in a more creative way to foster connection within the group.

Showing up does not only mean physically being present. When we show up we are fully here in body, mind, and spirit. This means we are fully connected to our experience, fully present in our connections with others, and fully aware of the context of our experience. We can be responsive rather than reactive, to both the people and actions or environment around us. We can be fully aware and fully experience the emotions we are feeling, while watching the dynamics of all that is happening around us and know that we too, are a part of those dynamics.

SHOW UP FOR LIFE AND LIFE SHOWS UP FOR YOU

The fact is that Life is everywhere. It is within us, it is all around us, it is right here in front, between, inside, outside and everywhere. Life is merely waiting for us to connect — to *re*-connect - with it in its entirety. Being present for all of the ups and downs, the beauty, the devastation, and the full range of rhythms and emotions makes the difference between living in black and white or living in full technicolour, multi-dimensional, full-sensory, surround-sound. When you truly show up, you can be open to seeing new possibilities for yourself and your life that may have eluded you if you were feeling stuck or blocked in some way. You can experience the vitality and vibrancy of life, the interconnectivity of it all, and the magic that happens when you allow yourself to be present.

QUESTIONS FOR REFLECTION:

1. **How are you showing up in your life right now?**
   For example: I do my best to allow myself to be fully present with whatever I am doing or whoever I am with at a moment in time. I show up with integrity, compassion, and openness to new ideas and creativity. I am also aware that I am not always able to do that.

2. **How are you showing up in your work?**
   For example: I honour the commitments I make and show up with the intention of being present. I am learning my limits of what I am able to accomplish in a day (a lesson that, personally, I seem to continue needing to learn over and over again) and when I need to take breaks to restore and renew my energy.

3. **How are you showing up in your relationships?**

   For example: When I am able to be fully present, I show up with caring, love, compassion and loyalty in my relationships. With my spouse I show up with love, commitment, and a desire to continue learning from and with one another through the ups and downs of this roller coaster called Life. With my children I do my best to be present for them and show up for them with a loving heart, attention, playfulness at times and firmly guiding at other times. I find I can more fully show up when I make space for quality time with the people I love.

4. **What gets in the way of you fully showing up at times?**

   For example: When I get overwhelmed with too much going on work-wise or family-wise I get stressed and my attention gets drawn away from the present moment. What also gets in my way is when I misunderstand intentions of others or when communication is muddled for whatever reason, I can get frustrated and experience myself as off balance.

5. **Imagine what could be possible if the obstacles were no longer there?**

   For example: If the obstacles were no longer there, I imagine the freedom I would experience within myself. My mind would be free of the clutter of self-criticism and I would be even more connected with my intuition and creativity. My relationships with the people I care about would thrive even more than they already do.

6. **What would you need to change within yourself to be more present in your life?**

   For example: I would need to transform some of the judgments I have of myself to make room for more self-compassion. I would also need to continue working on my awareness within each moment of my day. Awareness would include whatever is going on within me, of others and their experiences, and awareness within the context of whatever environment I am in. I would need to slow down more to truly be more present.

7. **Whatever you wrote as your response to the last question, re-write it again but in the present tense so that it reads as an action that you are taking.**

   For example: I am transforming some of the judgments I have of myself to make room for more self-compassion. I am continuing to work on my awareness within each moment of my day. This awareness includes whatever is going on within me, of others and their experiences, and awareness within the context of whatever environment I am in. I am slowing down more to truly be more present.

8. **What, if anything, was different when you wrote your response as a present action compared to your former response?**

   For example: When I read my response as a present tense action, I noticed my energy rising and I felt positive and hopeful about "the now" rather than the "maybe one day." Reading it in the present tense had more resonance for me than the first response.

To keep our faces toward change and **behave like free spirits** in the presence of fate is strength undefeatable.
- Helen Keller

8

Preparation for Showing Up

If you want to become more consciously aware of how you are showing up for your life, it is important to know the difference between when you actually do show up and when you do not. Noticing how you experience yourself when you are fully present and engaged in the moment, and how you experience yourself when you are not completely showing up is paramount to being more intentional about how you choose to more consciously show up in your life. You can prepare for this by first making the decision that you will show up today, starting your day with the intention of living fully, embracing the full spectrum of your experience at a moment in time. Hold onto the knowledge that your experience is not static and unchanging, but is constantly in flux from one moment to the next.

What do you have that you can be grateful for at this moment in time? Experiencing gratitude allows you to make the space to get into your being. Making space for silence, for meditation, for prayer; space to just be. It doesn't have to be a huge chunk of time either —

simply starting out with as little as three minutes a day will have an impact. When you give yourself the gift of making space, it makes a huge difference in how you show up.

CHECKLIST FOR SHOWING UP

☐ **Making Space**

1. **What are some of the ways that you can get yourself centred?**
   Some examples: deep breathing or other relaxation techniques, meditation, prayer, consciously slowing yourself down, affirmations, mantras, or setting intentions.

☐ **Connecting with Your Physical Presence**

2. **What are some ways you can get connected with your body through movement?**
   Some examples: Exercise, running, yoga, dancing, stretching, jumping, walking, or anything that gets you in your body and moving.

☐ **Setting Intentions for the Day**

3. **Ask yourself: "What will I create today?" "What do I need to do today?"**
   Make a list that includes what absolutely must happen and get done today, and make sure you include tasks that move you towards whatever your response was to the question of what you would like to create.

Personally, I am list person. I love the physicality of writing down with pen and paper all the things I need and want to accomplish in my day. I confess, I even add things to the list just to cross them off (and I am willing to bet that I'm not the only one who does that!). When you make the time to set your intentions about the day ahead, you are taking ownership of your day rather than your day taking ownership of you.

If you are checking your email and text messages as soon as you wake up in the morning, then you begin your day in response to others. You are reacting to what others' requests are of you, others' sharing their information with you or asking you about something. You become busy responding to other people's requests rather than being in charge of what the start of your day will be. You become engulfed in what others had as their priority, not you. This energetically sets the tone for the whole day. Try to intentionally leave your screens and phones aside for the first hour after you wake up in the morning and instead use this time for your own personal preparation to be fully present for your day. Notice what happens when you are able to do this.

☐ **Practice Gratitude**

4. **What are you grateful for today? Find a minimum of three to five things to be grateful for each day.**

Gratitude is all about finding something to be thankful for even in the midst of chaos and tragedy. The very act of searching for what you are grateful for creates new neural pathways in your brain and actually increases levels of serotonin and dopamine, those neurotransmitters that elevate your mood. So when my "to do" list is overflowing and my stress levels are high and I find myself having racing thoughts about everything and nothing, I pause to be grateful for my next breath. I can be grateful for sleep, for the homemade cookies on the counter lovingly made by my son, for the cup of coffee my husband brings to me every morning no matter what room I am in, for the love notes from my daughter. I can find countless things to be truly grateful for even in the midst of my own stress. It is in the finding of these things — pausing to take a moment to appreciate them — that the stress lessens, the body relaxes a little, and the bigger picture comes back into view.

ACTION STEPS

1. **What decision(s) are you willing to make right now about how you will change your morning so you are not simply in response mode but are more in charge of how your day will unfold?**

   For example: I will complete my morning ritual of stretching, breathing, prayer/meditation as well as eating my breakfast and making my 'to do' list for the day before even considering to check my phone and email for messages.

2. **What rituals will you put in place for your body movement each day?**

   For example: stretching, yoga, running, exercise bike, dancing, gym, or walking

3. **What practice will you put in place for your mind?**
   For example: making a list each morning, listening to an interesting podcast or webinar, reading a good book, expanding your knowledge on a certain topic, journaling about your ideas and learnings.

4. **What ritual will you commit to for your spiritual wellness?**
   For example: prayer, meditation, taking a walk in nature, yoga, tai chi, or other rituals for centring yourself.

The world is full of magic things, patiently waiting for our senses to grow sharper.
- W.B. Yeats

9

Presence: Developing Your Awareness

Much has been written about presence, about mindfulness and about being in the moment. What does it mean to be fully present and what are the benefits of it? When you are present, you are able to completely experience whatever is happening in a single moment in time. You become aware of all of the sounds, the energy in the room or place, the colours, the smells, the taste in your mouth; everything. Your senses are a wealth of information that relate to what is occurring at the exact place at an exact moment in time. When you are present and fully in the moment, your responses are relevant to whatever is happening right in front of you and around you. Try it!

EXERCISE FOR AWARENESS

Being Present with Your 5 Senses

Notice where you are at this exact moment in time. What do you see? Really look around you and see if you notice the obscure, tiny details, the colours, and the way the light shines and casts shadows.

Notice the sounds, even if it is "silent." When you really pay attention, what do you hear in the silence?

Now take a deep breath in through your nose and notice how you are breathing and what you are smelling.

Bring your attention to the texture and feel of what is around you. Allow your hands to move and feel the objects near you, feel your hands in your lap or touching your arms, noticing the temperature, the roughness or smoothness.

Bring your tongue to the roof of your mouth to stimulate your taste buds and notice what happens there.

Notice how time seems to slow down a bit when you allow yourself to really experience all of your senses. *You* slow down a bit when you do this.

Being Present With Your Feelings

To be fully present with your Self you also need to be fully accepting of who you are and whatever it is that you are experiencing at a moment in time. It is possible to be aware of your feelings and the way they shift and change from one moment to the next. Your feelings — your emotions — are also a source of information for you in the same way that your senses are. They help inform you about what is going on inside of you and how you are being impacted. For example, your sadness might be telling you about the hurt you feel about your perception of being alone, or about deserving to be treated with more respect, or about needing to experience more love, or any number of messages. Being present allows your feelings to simply be there without judgment. Notice how you tend to judge your feelings as "good feelings" or "bad feelings." You learned those classifications when you were young by how others responded to you when you were experiencing different emotions. Maybe you were scolded if you showed too much joy and happiness, maybe you were punished if you showed your frustration, or maybe you were not allowed to cry when you were feeling scared or sad. Depending how people responded to you, you learned to judge what emotions were acceptable or unacceptable to have or to display.

You can become more aware of the judgments you have about your emotions, for it is awareness that then allows you to choose something different. When you judge your emotions, the feelings often become bigger and more stuck than if you just let them be. When you are fully present with your emotions, you can give yourself permission to simply notice them. The greater challenge might be to also give yourself permission to accept them. Listen to what it is you might be needing or wanting at that moment in time. In doing so, you give yourself an opportunity to look underneath the emotion for the underlying need or message that it's offering.

Being Present With Your Thoughts

When you are fully present, you are able to notice your thoughts and what meaning you are giving to a moment in time. Knowing that your thoughts shift and change enables you to be more in charge of where you direct your thoughts and attention. You can learn to choose how you use your thoughts to support and nourish yourself, rather than to deprecate yourself. You can discover how thoughts feed your energy or deplete it. You can rally your thoughts to direct your intentions, your actions, and your decisions. Notice that you have all kinds of thoughts and beliefs about yourself, about others, and about the world around you. You can take an inner snapshot of your thoughts and beliefs at any moment in time and notice how many of these are actually not static or permanent but do change from one moment to the next.

Being Present With Your Expectations

You can become aware of expectations that you have at a moment in time and the impact those expectations might be having on your ability to be fully open and present; if your expectations are too high, then the natural process of what could happen may become blocked rather than unfolding. In the same way, if your expectations are too low this could also contribute to blocks that get in the way of your ability to be fully open to the possibilities of the present. Notice that you have expectations of yourself as well as expectations of other people. You even make all kinds of assumptions of what you think others expect from you, but how often do you actually check to see if those assumptions are accurate or not?

Being Present With Your Yearnings

All of this being present practice can be followed and linked to some very universal needs that every human being has, no matter how old they may be. You can be aware of your yearnings and notice what is it that you need in a moment, whether it be a need for love and belonging, safety, peace, freedom, validation, or something else that would help you to experience more harmony within yourself.

If you can be truly present with your Self and accept your internal experience at any moment in time, and also accept this experience with love and compassion, then you can be completely open to connecting with people at a much deeper level. Things shift from feeling like you only relate to others through discussions about superficial or easy topics, to really finding out what is happening at a deeper level with the people you meet. You can be present for your own experience when you are with others, and you can be present for others as they share their experience with you. In other words, it is possible for you to be aware of what is going on in every part of your present experience while holding space to also be fully present for another human being. You do not need to sacrifice one for the other.

Below is a diagram of Satir's iceberg metaphor. It shows all the parts of your internal experience at any given moment. You can use this as a map to guide your exploration and become more aware of what is going on in your experience. You may also use this to guide your curiosity about others' internal experience.

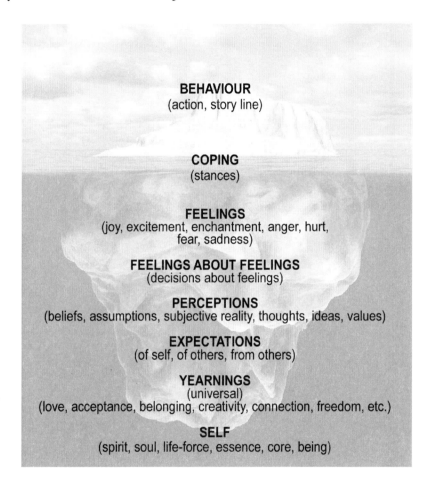

BEHAVIOUR
(action, story line)

COPING
(stances)

FEELINGS
(joy, excitement, enchantment, anger, hurt,
fear, sadness)

FEELINGS ABOUT FEELINGS
(decisions about feelings)

PERCEPTIONS
(beliefs, assumptions, subjective reality, thoughts, ideas, values)

EXPECTATIONS
(of self, of others, from others)

YEARNINGS
(universal)
(love, acceptance, belonging, creativity, connection, freedom, etc.)

SELF
(spirit, soul, life-force, essence, core, being)

© See: Satir, V., Banmen, J., Gerber, J., & Gomori, M. 1991. The Satir Model: Family Therapy and Beyond. Palo Alto, CA: Science and Behavior Books. Inc.

QUESTIONS TO GUIDE EXPLORATION OF YOUR "ICEBERG"

There are many ways to explore your iceberg. You might choose to use the present moment to check in with yourself and increase your awareness of what is happening in your internal experience at a given moment. Or you might be curious to process what was happening in your experience with a past event. You can explore the impact of events when you were triggered, and you can also explore impacts of events when you were in your bliss and joy. The choice is yours.

For the purpose of practicing right now, decide whether you would like to focus on the present moment in time, a recent event, or an event from your past. Once you have decided what you will explore, go through the following questions and allow yourself to sit with each one so that you can peel back the layers underneath your initial responses.

1. **Behaviour: Briefly describe the context of the event. What were you doing? What happened?**

2. **Coping Stance(s): If you were experiencing any stress at the time, what survival coping stance were you using?**

   Some examples: Were you denying your own experience or sacrificing your own needs to placate someone else (Placating)? Were you finding fault with the other person and blaming them (Blaming)? Were you cut off from your feelings, ignoring what was going on for you and others and trying to problem-solve (Super-reasonable)? Or were you doing your best to distract yourself from what was going on (Irrelevant), either by avoiding it altogether, cracking jokes, or making comments that were completely irrelevant to what was happening at the time?

3. **What feelings did you experience during this time? Use words that describe your emotions.**

   Some examples: angry, scared, happy, excited, sad, confused, joyful, frustrated, anxious, compassionate.

4. **How did you feel about having each of these feelings? What other emotions came up for you based on the feelings you were experiencing?**

   Some examples: shame and guilt about feeling angry, angry and sad about feeling scared, excited about feeling happy, nervous and happy about feeling excited, confusion and shame about feeling sad, annoyed about feeling confused, happy about feeling joyful

5. **How did you see yourself and what did you believe about you at that moment?**

   Some examples: I saw myself as... powerful, powerless, lonely, surrounded, big, small, significant, insignificant, weak, strong, misunderstood, helpless

6. **What were you thinking about others at the time (either others who were a part of any interactions that may have taken place, or other people in general)?**
Some examples: Others are... better than me, worse than me, powerful, powerless, trustworthy, untrustworthy, big, small, significant, insignificant, weak, strong, right, wrong.

7. **What did you believe about your world in that moment?**
Some examples: The world is... safe, unsafe, beautiful, ugly, peaceful, chaotic, predictable, scary.

8. **What are some of the expectations you had of yourself in that moment?**
   Some examples: I should have remained calm. I should have spoken up for myself. I should have been more prepared.

9. **What did you expect from others?**
   Some examples: They should have known better. They should have helped out more. They should have understood what I meant. They should have remained calm.

10. **What is your guess about what they expected from you?**
Some examples: I think they expected me to lead the way, to remain calm and grounded, and to know the answers.

11. **What were you yearning for at that moment? What was it that you really needed**
at the time?
Some examples: safety, peace, connection, love, belonging, freedom, validation

12. **How did you experience your connection with your life energy and essence at that moment? As you reflect on your experience, what internal resources are you aware of now that may have helped you through the moment?**

For example: When I was in my reaction, I was not very connected with that peaceful, joyful place inside of me and did not experience the flow of my life energy. As I reflect on my experience, I am now aware of how I used my tenacity to not give up, and my resource of caring and love for wanting to resolve what was going on.

Peace within, peace
between, peace **among**.
 - Virginia Satir

10

Self: Finding the Container Within

Imagine a time when you experienced indescribable joy and peace, connected with your soul and the universe. Maybe it was a fleeting moment, or maybe it lasted longer. Maybe it is challenging to think of moments like this, but I assure you, you have had some no matter what circumstances you have experienced in your life. I think of moments like these and can find many, both brief and longer, like when reaching the summit of a mountain after an arduous hike and experiencing that flicker of awe looking over the vastness of the landscape before me; or the moments right after my children were born — after the physical and emotional work of labour and pushing; or when listening to music so beautiful that I am moved to tears. It may even be what initially appears mundane, then suddenly seems miraculous to behold — like watching an elderly couple so in love with each other that they are lost in one another's gaze, or listening to the rain falling as it creates percussive beats, or momentarily noticing the way the light shines and dances through the tree branches. The experience of these moments is difficult to describe in words because words are so limiting when every cell in my body is vibrating and resonating with some universal Truth about who we are in the bigger picture of Life.

PAYING ATTENTION TO YOUR BODY WISDOM

These moments are gifts; gifts that remind us of who we really are underneath our ways of coping and how we have learned to get by in the world. If you can think of some of these moments that you have had, pay attention to what happens in your body as you think of them. Really notice what happens in your chest, your heart, your stomach, your head, your breathing, and the space within you. Even though the moment you are thinking of has happened in the past, by allowing yourself to get in touch with the memory you also allow your body to experience the memory's impact in the present. That place inside of you that holds onto the wisdom held within the experiences is the container within. This is the part that is kept and is always available for you to connect with, even when there is chaos around you. The container within is a space of refuge, a space of connection, a space of wisdom, and a space that you can consciously cultivate. It is this space that truly allows you to be present and show up for all moments of your life.

SPACE THAT CONNECTS

For just a moment, think of spaces in general and how they are necessary and essential to distinguish and separate things. For example, it is because of the spaces between the notes that we hear music; the spaces that separate one note from the next and yet connect the notes to one another to create the whole of the musical piece. Think of the spaces between each breath — the still point between our inhalation and exhalation — that connect our rhythm of breathing to allow us to continue living. Our living space is even made up of smaller spaces that distinguish the living room from the kitchen from the bedroom. A forest is made up from a multitude of trees separated by spaces between them. There are countless examples of various spaces that ultimately distinguish and separate yet connect to form something bigger. That distinction of space is also what connects each of us to everything.

The space within us is what connects us with the whole of our life; without the space, there would be no way of connecting one moment to the next. They would tumble together. We can be consciously aware of this container within ourselves; this container of space. It is the place of stillness and peace that exists no matter what, and a place that we want to connect with more. It is safety within ourselves. This is not a place where we are closed off from the rest of the world: connecting within does not negate what is happening outside (or "without"). But it can be our refuge in the storm of chaos. Our place of solace as we connect with a moment of peace, of inner wisdom, the divine nature within ourselves, and with what is so much bigger than us, yet a part of us. Space to be. Space to breathe. Space to listen to the wisdom that is within and around us. Space to connect. When we are learning to live fully in the present, it is this space that allows us to stay with the present, to show up for the more challenging experiences of life, to foster calm and trust, and to live a complete experience. Perhaps there is much more to space than we realize. Space is far from empty. In fact, it is in the connection with this space that we can also allow ourselves to be fully present in our lives.

QUESTIONS FOR REFLECTION

1. **Draw a picture, write a poem, find a metaphor or find a photo that depicts the container of space within yourself.**
   For example: I picture a beautiful, multi-coloured sunset over the ocean. Or a strong radiant light that pulsates from within and spreads out towards all.

2. **What are some words that describe this space for you?**

   For example: peaceful, bliss, harmony, empty yet full, love-filled, divine

3. **How can you be more conscious in cultivating this space within you?**

   For example: I find that when I am practicing gratitude, praying or meditating, I am nurturing this space within myself. I can make time to consciously connect with this space each day, pausing to place my hands on my core or over my heart and breathing into this space, imagining light within myself. I can also make greater efforts to find moments to be in nature where it is easier for me to connect with this space.

In the midst of my darkness **I found the sun within myself**.

- Albert Camus

11

Presence in Fear, Devastation and Sorrow

Very often when we think of being present, we associate it with being in a calm, positive, pleasant environment and circumstances. Certain contexts, such as meditation, yoga, walking in nature, sitting at the beach watching the waves of the ocean, playing attentively with our children, or spending quality time with someone we love tend to lend themselves to a higher possibility of increased presence. But there are also other moments — moments of chaos, fear, devastation and sorrow when we might want to be anything but present — that in fact, lend to our ability to be present in a way that seems to slow time right down. There is much we can learn from these moments and how we show up for them when they present themselves to us in their oh-so-unpredictable ways. I would like to share with you the story of one of these experiences from my own life.

STRANGERS IN THE FACE OF TRAGEDY

"Just look into my eyes, look at me".

I remember hearing him say that as calmness swept over me and I looked deep into my husband's eyes. I settled a little, my shoulders let go of some of the immense tension and my mind came back to awareness of where I was. I took some deep breaths as my body regained its normal regulation. We are in this together. Whatever happens, we are together.

I was holding the hand of a dying boy whom I had never met until that night. Rod, my husband, and I had "hijacked" a passenger bus so we could get the boy to the nearest hospital.

We were in Peru, having recently completed our multi-day trek to Macchu Picchu and were enjoying some other areas of the country on our backpacking adventure. The night had begun with us travelling from Arequipa to Nazca on an overnight bus so we could experience the infamous Nazca lines. It was shortly after midnight and I was arriving into sleep when there was a blood-curdling scream from the woman in front with the driver. A loud bang followed, along with a sudden jolt of the bus, then the squealing of tires and out of control skidding along the dangerous, winding mountain road that had no barrier to prevent going over the edge. In that moment, I believed with every cell in my body that we were all about to die. I had no idea what had just happened. I thought for sure the bus was going to go over the high cliffs we were driving along and we would fall to our peril. My body jolted awake. Suddenly I was very much present. My heart was pounding. My thoughts raced about how this was completely out of my control. Then the words: an expletive being the first one, and then "Please God, please God, please God — help us". Then a flicker of a thought, "This is going to devastate my parents."

I remember this so clearly; the clarity of being so certain that I was not yet ready to die, and on the other hand, accepting that this — my death — was going to happen and was about to happen. I find the order of my words and thoughts interesting and quite telling. When faced with true imminent threat of death, my thoughts and fears unraveled at high speed through the fear and anger in the expletive, followed by invocation of help from a higher power, and then compassion for how this would impact my family. This was the depth of my desire to Live.

The bus came to a stop after what seemed like ages but was probably only a few seconds. It was as though every fraction of a second was imperative to the slow-motion reality of what was happening. All at once, there was confusion, fear, and anxiety over what had just occurred.

Our bus had been involved in a head-on collision with another vehicle. After moments of stillness, some of the passengers got off the bus to see what had happened. One came running back onto the bus with the energy of frantic terror:

"Is there a doctor on the bus?!!!!!!"

Nobody answered.

And then, Rod stood up. He was not a doctor, but he had experience as a paramedic. That would do if nobody else could help. I remained stuck to my seat for a few minutes, feeling unable to move as I watched my husband walk off the bus and into the dark abyss of this nightmare. Then I suddenly came back into my full experience and told myself that I needed to get out there to see how I could help. My compassion for human life had bumped my own terror out of the way and propelled me off the bus to see what I could do. There had been five people in the car that our bus had hit. Rod checked all of their pulses;

all but one were dead. There was a young boy in the back who was still breathing — very slow, laboured, and raspy breaths. But he was breathing. Rod took charge of the situation, involving other passengers from the bus to help extricate the boy from the crumpled metal that had once been a car.

A police officer had entered the scene at some point. He was in the middle of the road directing traffic. I assumed an ambulance was well on its way. We approached the police officer to ask when the ambulance would arrive. He stared at us somewhat blankly and said there would be no ambulance. What?!!! It was then that we also noticed that our bus driver and the other staff member had fled the scene. Literally fled! They hopped on board another passing bus and left the rest of us passengers — a combination of local and international travellers - stranded in the middle of the Peruvian desert. No ambulance meant this boy would certainly die. I remember Rod and I became very focused and very present as we communicated our determination to get the boy to the nearest hospital by any means possible. With the help of a fellow passenger who translated for us, we ordered the police officer to stop the next bus that passed by. He did. We asked him to tell the bus driver that we needed to get to the nearest hospital. He did. Very carefully, Rod talked us through lifting him onto the bus. We did.

I did not care that I had left my backpack with all of my belongings on the bus we had just left. At that moment, it became very clear that Life was so much more important than any belongings, belongings that could be replaced. Rod and I held this unconscious boy as the bus, filled with locals, drove to the nearest town hospital. I held the boy's hand and talked gently and quietly with him. Even though I did not speak his language, I wanted him to know that he was not alone and that we were right there with him. It was in those moments that it became clear that Connection can be experienced between and among complete strangers in the face of tragedy. Nobody on that commandeered bus complained that the bus driver was taking them completely off their route of travel and delaying their arrival wherever their final destination was. In fact, many shared their gratitude and appreciation to Rod and I for doing what we could to try and save this child.

My panic started to build. The adrenaline of having survived what I thought would have been my death, and now trying to help this dying boy caught up with me. Rod saw it in my eyes and in my breathing.

"Just look into my eyes, look at me."

That is all it took to bring me back. To bring me back into focus and connection. Connection with my husband. Connection with the boy. Connection with the energy of concern and caring on the bus.

Maybe it was 40 minutes, or maybe it was an hour, but eventually we arrived at the hospital. I had imagined there would be a team of doctors waiting expectantly with a gurney ready to whisk him off, ready to save his life. Having been inside plenty of emergency rooms in the past and having witnessed all that transpires in one, I had assumed that this would be no different. I had assumed wrong. My expectations of a first class North American emergency room had not prepared me for the reality. There was nobody. It was the middle of the night and the building seemed nearly deserted. I ran inside and down the hallway to find a doctor, finally encountering someone slowly sauntering towards me. My rushed, urgent energy certainly did not match what was going on in this place. A small team of doctors and nurses did come to get the boy. They thanked us, and took him inside. My heart sank as I realized that this hospital and its doctors did not have what was needed to save this boy's life. We had done all that we could do and were told that they had him now and that we could go. It all seemed so unfinished for me though. Going was not such an easy thing to do when I wanted to be with this boy and make sure he was not alone. Yet it became clear by the abandoned halls and the bus driver waiting for us by the doors that maybe there really was nothing else that we could do at the present moment.

Rod and I had not really thought past the present moment, and we were now confronted with our new present moment. The moment when the bus driver, without saying a word, motioned that he would drive us all the way to where we had commandeered the bus in the first place. I have no idea how much time had already passed, but I do know that it must have been at least a couple of hours. Yet, all the passengers were still there where we had left them along with the stranded bus, with no news of how or when we would be rescued. We re-joined our group of fellow passengers and responded to their questions of what had happened with the boy. Everyone shared their anger and frustration with what had happened (our bus driver was clearly at fault in this accident). Everyone shared their compassion for the five passengers in the car. Everyone shared their food and water with one another.

The cool desert night began to warm as the sun rose. I remember the array of colours in that sunrise in the desert and even took a photo to capture the stark contrast between the beauty of the sunrise and the tragedy of what had happened that night.

With daylight came the arrival of a rescue truck, to untangle the mass of metal and extricate the bodies from the car. Still no word of when we would be rescued. We stood by, each of us with our own experience of sadness, sorrow, anger and frustration as we witnessed these four bodies laid out side by side on the desert sand before being covered by a tarp. We kept asking the rescue squad if they had any news about the boy but we were not given an answer.

The coroner arrived on the scene, and the bus driver who had fled returned with his crew to be interviewed by the coroner about what happened. One of the passengers who spoke both English and Spanish went to stand nearby in order to overhear the interrogation. She came marching back up the sandy hill in an outrage saying that the bus driver had lied about the whole incident to make it seem like the accident was the fault of the other car. The skid marks on the road told a different story. The eyewitness accounts of the other passengers told a different story. I marched right back down that hill along with a passenger whom I asked to translate for me, and I told the coroner that I wanted to file an official report too about what happened. He took my statement. The local passengers from the bus told me afterward that the bus company likely had already bribed the police and the coroner to write a report in their favour.

We then learned that the boy had died from his injuries. We were not told anything else about what had happened with him, only that he had not survived. We all wept. This diverse conglomerate of human beings, thrown together by a tragic event, comforted one another through their own forms of grief. A sense of connectedness and community formed at that moment in time.

Finally another bus did arrive to pick us all up and take us to our intended destination. We were quiet as we boarded the bus — all relieved to be rescued but still very much in process over what we had just been through. There were a few times when we all seemed to be simultaneously triggered by this new driver's speed around the corners, or changing lanes into oncoming traffic to pass a slower vehicle (which is the action that had led to that tragic accident). A collective intake of breath, a cry of "do you not realize what we have all just been through?". Each one of us more sensitive than usual, and barely out of the tragedy of the night before. I had not realized how much tension I had been holding until we finally arrived in Nazca and checked into our hostel.

We were all profoundly brought together by this shared event — connected more intimately than had we merely been passengers en route to a destination — that took us beyond what may have stayed at the level of surface conversation, where people ask 'where are you from?'. We were all impacted differently, yet the connection forged was deeper because of those eight hours spent in the desert.

The value of life was gained from that bus ride in Peru. How Life is bigger than any of us; how embracing life also means accepting the inevitability of death, being granted the power of connection, and the honour of what I call 'withness' — being with another when they are suffering and holding hope for them — and appreciating how there are still moments of beauty and grace in the midst of tragedy.

To show up for the devastation, I had to find refuge in the container within; connecting with that still point of peace that is contained within me no matter what is going on in the rest of my experience. I did this by taking breaths to slow myself down and placing my hand on my heart for compassion. Looking into my husband's eyes also allowed me to slow down and experience the grounding that connection with someone safe can bring. Showing up for Self, maintaining connection with others, and holding onto hope allowed me to be engaged in the full breadth of that night's experience. We can hold the space within ourselves to be strong enough to go to the vulnerable, scary places within us because we know we want something different. We can hold the space within us even when there is chaos all around us. Finding the still point — that still space within that is ours alone to connect with and to come home to — creates a refuge from which to experience the beauty and gifts in devastation.

Every experience that you have
with another human being gives you a
new opportunity to
experience yourself and to make
new connections.
- Jennifer Nagel

12

Relationships: The Container Between

Building trust and rapport in any kind of relationship and the way in which you use your Self in relationships is paramount for any kind of depth. How do you create a space of safety, acceptance, and love with and for others? How you show up for yourself and for others impacts the container that you create between you and those people with whom you spend time.

Every experience that you have with another human being gives you a new opportunity to experience yourself and to make new connections. You were born already hard-wired to connect with others, and your connections with others literally impact the development and growth of your brain.

CURRENT RELATIONSHIPS AND YOUR ENERGY

When you think about your relationships that you currently have in your life, you may notice that there are some that nurture your spirit and enhance your energy. You may also notice that there are some that seem to suck the energy right out of you, leaving you feeling depleted after spending time with those people. Pay attention to how your energy is impacted in each interaction you have with others. Notice the times when you feel fully engaged, present and alive versus the times when you are barely there, not paying attention, disengaged or even repelled. As an adult, you do have choice in which relationships you want to nurture and to offer your time. You can become more conscious in the creation of the container that holds the unique energy between you and another. Every one of your relationships has parts that belong uniquely between only two people. For example, my relationship with my mother has aspects that are unique between the two of us, different from the unique relationship between my father and I, and the unique relationship between my sister and I. Each one of my friendships has unique shared memories and qualities to them. How we are in our relationships impacts the way we meet or don't meet our yearnings for connection, belonging, intimacy and love.

CONTRIBUTING TO THE CONTAINER

You can reflect on how you are showing up in your relationships with the people in your life and what your contribution is in co-creating the container that holds the unique energy of each relationship. You can explore all forms of relationships in this manner, including family members, friends, clients, colleagues, acquaintances, and each person with whom you meet or interact. Each container will be different and what you bring to one may be the reverse of what another asks of you.

I desire to bring my best Self to all areas of my life but like many others, I can struggle with that when it comes to the people closest to me. How do I create that container for my children, for my husband, for my friends and extended family? This is curious since when I consider the container I aim to provide for each of my clients in therapy sessions and for the groups of participants in the workshops that I facilitate, I know with absolute confidence that I am able to be fully present and show up to provide a safe, trusting and loving container that allows them to be present for their process. Why is it that I sometimes struggle with those nearest and dearest to me, and am not always offering my best Self in those relationships? There seems to be more heightened sensitivity and triggers within the context of those relationships and maybe because these are the people nearest and dearest to me, there is a different standard of expectations that I hold for them. When expectations are not met there is some kind of reaction and this reaction will naturally trigger a response from others. Perhaps we need to take a closer look at how our experiences in the families we grew up in play into our present-day expectations in our present-day relationships.

FAMILY DYNAMICS

Families are our first social group. Our first experiences of being cared for — or not — are in the families where we grow up. Our first experiences shape how we function in a social group and we carry these learnings with us into our lives where they impact our relationships. If we find a partner and have children together, we each bring with us what we learned from our respective families. No two families are alike. There is not a single other family on this planet that has had the same life experiences or same impacts as another. This can create huge areas of tension and disagreement when raising children. Different ideas and values about parenting, discipline, and how families "should be" emerge quickly when you are raising your own children and have to blend somebody else's ideas with your own. Children are born as unique individuals and develop their sense of self and their place in the world based on impacts from how they are cared for as children. Raising children requires people to come together to establish a new container — the unique energy and dynamics, the good, the bad, the challenges and triumphs that exist in the one-of-a-kind container of family. As we develop in this first social group, we are subject to all the pushes and pulls of an emerging container and all its peculiarities and habits.

Parenting has probably been one area that has been the most challenging for my husband and I to navigate together. It was all well and good for us to share our dreams of how we wanted to raise our children, the values we wished to share with them, and our ideas of what "being together as a family" could look like. However, the Dream and the Reality don't seem to necessarily agree at times. Funny how children don't just fit into the mould of our expectations! Each child truly is their own, unique person and on the one hand it is truly remarkable to witness the development of their personalities and ideas and opinions, while on the other hand it is sometimes downright crazy-making as they remind us of their independence and their own will when they do not simply listen and do what they are asked.

We do not differ in what we want for our children, but there are times when we do disagree on "the how" part of attaining or providing it. For example, there are times when Rod wants immediate consequences for our children's misbehaviour and with a raised voice he will demand whatever it is they need to do. I, personally, have a tendency either to try and have a collaborative discussion with the children to hear each of their points of view and feelings about what happened, or when that fails miserably due to heightened emotions, I might raise my voice in an attempt to be heard. I might also walk away and let them stay with the struggle of figuring out how to make it work (as long as they are not throttling each other as a way of "working it out"). Now this can get really messy if we are both around at the same time. Can you imagine how confusing it might be for the kids with each parent reacting so differently? Not to mention, the added stress and tension of both parents not necessarily agreeing on how the other is responding?

My husband and I also sometimes disagree on the best way to teach our children to stand up for themselves. Again, we do not differ in what we want for our children, but we differ on how to work at attaining what we hope for them. So how do we deal with these differences? Let me start by saying it's a work in progress. We may not see things the same way, but we need to hear each other on a deeper level. What I mean by that is I want to hear how my husband sees it, where his feelings are coming from, and acknowledge his point of view. In the same way, I want him to hear how I see it, where my feelings are coming from, and acknowledge my point of view. We need to both experience being heard by the other. This does not resolve the situation, but it allows us to have more understanding of where each of us is coming from and starts getting us back on track, working together as a team in parenting.

The next part of our process is getting back to the root of what we want for our children and sharing more collaboratively our ideas of ways that we can work together. We explore our values and express what is truly important to us, which then allows us to open up to new decisions of how we want to be different, both with each other and with our children. When we can resolve our differences in this way, it lends to a more harmonious household. This also impacts our children in a positive way. They seem to get along better and their fights don't escalate to the degree that they do when we have conflict over our differences.

As I have already said, this is a work in progress as it is inevitable that differences will continue to arise as we navigate the various phases of life. What we do with those differences is what will determine whether we learn from each other and grow together, or whether we merely go into our individual coping.

I believe that families and all the ways we learn to survive in relationship with others — the ways we learn to protect ourselves and the ways we learn to get our needs met — provide the mirror and opportunity for us to grow. If we had no obstacles in our way, no triggers, no reactivity, no struggles or challenges, I don't think we would notice our growth to the same extent that we do when we learn how to overcome these obstacles and challenges.

ACKNOWLEDGING AND EXPERIENCING THE CHALLENGES

We end up being challenged the most in our families and close relationships because there is a tension that exists when we are inside the very container that we are also trying to create. We have our ideas and expectations of what the container needs to be and try so hard to impose those ideas — with absolutely positive intentions — but sometimes our efforts fall short. Those close to us also have their ideas and expectations of what the container needs to be, and the tension increases, triggering our stress response.

When my daughter comes home from school crying about how mean some of her friends were that day, the container between us allows for her to share and express her feelings, to be accepted and loved by me, for me to be with her in her pain without allowing the pain to suck me in to where I react or try to "problem-solve" right away. The container allows one to witness and experience vulnerability and chaos. Holding the space. The container has room for it all — the agony and the ecstasy and everything in between. That does not mean the container stores it all, but the safety of the container allows for every aspect of the experience to be expressed and received with love and acceptance. By holding it all in an energy of love and acceptance, whatever is in the space is transformed. Because the expression has not been judged, it is permitted to be transformed. The experience, itself, changes because it has not been shut down or pushed aside or made light of. It has not been suppressed or ridiculed or negated. The "withness" of that relational container holds tension, holds vulnerability, holds love, and holds hope, and by holding these things, it allows for something new to emerge such as new possibilities, new hope, and new opportunities.

However, there are those times when, despite my best intentions, I might not be holding the space of the container in ways that allow for that sacred "withness" to occur. In other words, those times when I do get sucked into my daughter's pain and respond or react differently. We can sometimes get caught up in our own reactions when we experience the people we care about struggling with their own painful challenges. Those are the times when I might go straight into problem-solving mode, wanting to "fix" it and find solutions with the most positive intentions of hoping to help her feel better. Or I might express my own frustration and disappointment in what happened with her friends that day, supporting my daughter's experience. I suspect we are all prone to doing this with the people we hold near and dear to us. However, brainstorming ways to assert oneself more or how to respond to friends who are mean or advising to find nicer friends is not what might be actually needed at that particular moment in time.

What ends up happening with my daughter is that she does not feel fully heard and understood if she is not given the space to fully express what is going on for her. She will then say something like, "You just don't understand," or "Never mind," or "I don't want to talk about it anymore." Furthermore, if I am in problem-solving mode then I might even be doing her a disservice by taking away from her own learning of how to work through issues with her friends. The end result is that my intentions of showing love and caring toward her fall short.

If I can hold the space and just be present for her, to listen and really hear what is going on for her, then when she is ready to explore what she wants and needs to do in relation to her friends, I can listen to her ideas and help her cultivate new possibilities of how she would like to be within herself and in her friendships. The container allows for holding the space for creative collaboration and for the connection together which allows for the experience of being seen, heard, accepted, loved, and feeling safe.

HOLDING THE SPACE WITH LOVE AND ACCEPTANCE

As I carry the desire and hope to bring my best Self to the people I love most, I know that when I am able to hold that space of the sacred container then the magic of transformation unfolds. When I can be with my son with love and acceptance when he is expressing his anger with his fists and his words — when I can acknowledge his disappointment and hurt rather than reacting to his behaviours — the behaviour itself changes because the deeper yearnings and emotions have been seen and acknowledged for what they are.

When I react to the behaviours and only focus on what it is he has done wrong, it seems to escalate the very behaviours I am wanting him to stop. For example, if my voice is raised as I sternly tell him that it is not appropriate to hurt his sister, I am missing an opportunity to find out what is happening for him that is contributing to his actions or hurtful words. If I am missing this, he is not experiencing himself as understood and chances are pretty high that his behaviours will escalate and get even worse instead of better in that moment. His behaviours escalate, my frustration and anger escalate, and I am sure you can imagine that it is not a pretty picture of a "nice, happy family." When I am in my own reactions and contributing to the escalation of tensions and conflicts within my family, feelings of guilt, shame and frustration arise in me. That internal critic of mine comes along to tell me that I am doing a terrible job as a parent and that I am failing miserably at dealing with this whole mess. What I am really yearning for in those moments is peace, safety, and for all of us to truly hear one another in a way that contributes to our connection. I suppose I am wanting us all to do a better job of loving one another.

Now, of course it is not alright for my son to be hurting his sister and limits do need to be set. However, what I am saying here is that when he does experience himself as heard and understood, his energy shifts and his behaviours change. He visibly relaxes his shoulders and his yelling might turn into tears of frustration or sadness or both. When he is understood in this way and is helped to name what is really going on for him, then we can look at alternative ways to handle his frustrations and disappointments when they come up. The repair work can really only be done in the context of love, safety, acceptance, and connection. When all of this is cultivated within the container of the relationship between myself and anyone I am in relationship with, whether it be my son, my daughter, my husband, my friends or colleagues, then there can exist the possibility for building deeper connections as we repair, restore and grow from our experience.

ACCEPTING OTHERS FOR WHO THEY ARE UNDERNEATH THEIR BEHAVIOURS

We are each having our own human experience, and this experience impacts how we are with ourselves and in relationship with others. How can we accept people for who they are at their core even when we may dislike or strongly disagree with how they are behaving?

When I am consciously working on being centred within my Self, I am experiencing my own love, acceptance, safety, and connection. I am in touch with a sense of oneness with everything and a connection with the Divine, which I experience as love in its purest form and something far greater than myself. I am aware of my expectations for myself and can accept others for who they are at their essence rather than for what they are doing in their behaviours. Holding hope for another human being means we have to truly know hope. I hold onto the knowledge and the belief that change is possible. My feelings remain very positive, compassionate, excited, and hopeful rather than reactive. I have no need for coping or reacting because I am centred in Self and all of this is reflected in my behaviour. The ways in which I use my face, my body, my eyes, my voice and the things I say reflect my internal experience of being connected with the essence of who I am. When I can do this within myself, nourishing the sacred container between myself and another human being becomes much more natural.

STRUGGLES WITHIN THE CONTAINER

When I am working with clients or facilitating a workshop, I am the one creating that safe container. I am responsible for holding the safety, love and acceptance for the group, and the boundaries are much more clearly defined. The container allows for people to dig deep and go to those vulnerable scary places because they know they want change and can believe that change is possible.

The difference when I am with my family is that I am actually inside the container — the container of my family. It is far easier to be slightly on the periphery within the container in order to be a witness for others and to use my strengths and intuition to observe and foster others on their journeys of growth and discovery. The bigger struggle comes from being inside the container within a system of several people — my family members — all involved in trying to create it. Each person within the family has their own ideas of what that container needs to be. That means the container is less clearly defined because it is constantly in flux.

The gift that is being offered to us if we choose is to acknowledge the challenges when they arise and to experience all of it; the pain, the joy, the anguish, the frustration, the hurt, the sadness, the triumphs. Experience the roller coaster adventure of the ups and downs of our relationships, noticing when we are off-centre or receiving it as a gift to use for our growth and learning. It may be that having the opportunity to grow through relationship is what allows us to cultivate our best Self. It is a practice field for honing our ability to know when we are not fully connected with our essence; a regular opportunity to hone the ability to return to that connection where our love and acceptance flow freely. For it is true that when we are connected in that place, we can be more present in our relationships. The container of relationship makes us more able to be ourselves, which in turn, offers more to the container of relationship. The container between us becomes nourished and supported as we navigate each unique relationship in our life.

QUESTIONS FOR REFLECTION

1. **As you reflect on the various relationships you have with the people in your life, which are the ones that feed and refresh your energy? Describe what it is about each of these people that enhances your life.**

    For example: As I reflect on specific individuals whom I feel refreshed and energized by when I interact with them, I notice that each one of them seems to have their own vitality and a desire for ongoing growth and learning. There is a mutual support that exists between myself and each of these people in which they are there for me when I am struggling, and I am there for them when they are struggling. We are also there for each other to celebrate in our triumphs and joys. These people have a sense of their own responsibility for themselves and are authentic in the way they show up in their own relationships with themselves and others.

2. **Which relationships in your life currently seem to deplete your energy and leave you feeling exhausted? Describe what it is about each of these people that seems to take up a lot of your energy.**

    For example: As I reflect on specific individuals whom I feel drained and depleted by after interacting with them, I notice that these people seem to lack motivation to grow and change. They seem to stay stuck in their stories of complaints and victimhood without really making efforts to do their part to change their story. Our interactions seem to be very one-sided, with them taking little to no interest in what is going on for me in my own life.

3. **What choices do you have in how you want to be in each of your relationships? How would you like to contribute to the co-creation of the unique container that exists between you and each person in your life?**

    For example: I do have choice in whom I spend time with and I can choose to spend more time with those people who enhance my life energy. I can consciously cultivate my relationships with those people, and can consciously choose whom to spend less time with or to no longer be with. I would like to contribute to the unique container of each of my relationships by showing up with authenticity, compassion and love. I can also be more aware of my own internal boundaries within each of my relationships and know when I am safe to be vulnerable and open, and when it is unsafe for me to share with certain people in my life.

At any given moment you are always in some kind of **relationship** with **yourself**, with **others** and with the **world**. You never exist in isolation.

- Jennifer Nagel

13

The Container of Community

At any given moment you are always in some kind of relationship with yourself, with others and with the world. You never exist in isolation. You are not alone even when there is nobody around you, for you have your own internalized experience of your relationship with yourself and others. During the first part of your life, you were raised within the family and community you were born into. We do not really have a choice in that while our caregivers pass along their values, beliefs and rules for getting by and thriving in life — our upbringing. As we get older our social world starts to expand and we have more choice about the friends we like to be with, our choice of extra-curricular activities, hobbies and clubs, and what actions we take in the world. We begin to create our own community. Community holds potential for belonging, connection, safety, love, freedom, independence, validation, and all our yearnings to be met. It offers potential for thriving, growth, and learning. Yet, sometimes our fears of not fitting in, of being judged, of being unlovable, or of not being enough get in our way of fully thriving. And sometimes it is not one's perceived fear but the reality when certain communities do judge and condemn if there's a perception of non-conformity. I have had many clients come with impacts from being emotionally, physically, mentally, or spiritually abused by their communities. Their sense of betrayal, hurt, anger and injustice is enormous as well as confusion for what happened; sometimes, they were simply being their unique Selves.

STARTING FROM WITHIN TO HEAL CONNECTIONS

Community can contribute to feeding and nourishing our soul or it can contribute to damaging our connection with self, others, and the world. When the latter has occurred, the healing work starts from within. A person must heal the emotional and spiritual wounds that have been carried and impacted their connection. This process includes: acceptance of what happened in the past (and acceptance does not mean liking or condoning what happened); forgiveness and letting go (which does not mean forgetting, but does mean that we no longer need to be emotionally triggered and can learn from it in order to move on); and making a new decision for ourselves, then making the changes necessary to support that new decision.

But when we have a loving, supportive, caring community surrounding us, it creates the container for us to experience life more fully and with more authentic connection. Greater authenticity allows for more meaningful relationships allows for more meaningful relationships, more depth in our connections, and more joy in our experience. We were meant to have love and joy in our lives. Authentic connection also allows for increased compassion and more capacity to be there for one another. In other words, it yields a more fulfilling life. When we experience ourselves as fulfilled we have an abundance of energy, creativity and intuition to contribute and connect with others, our community, and society at large. Authentic connection within community also provides the container for us to be supported in our intimate relationships with others.

NURTURED BY THE CONTAINER OF COMMUNITY

In spite of Rod being in the hospital fighting for his life, and me working full-time while pregnant with our first child, we were still able to be there for one another and with one another. He was just as supportive of me emotionally as I was of him. I remember being asked about who took care of me while I was busy caring for my husband. It seemed an odd question that did not resonate at all for me given that my experience was that my husband and I were continuing to care for one another; I felt his strength and support even when he was physically weak and feeling like crap.

Looking back now, I see that experiencing our support for one another was fostered and nurtured by the container of our community. The community that was bringing us home-cooked meals to physically nourish us, the community that was praying for us, the community that was sending love and healing energy our way, the community that ensured we were cared for in all the ways that we might need. Experiencing that container to its fullest emphasized and helped me learn the importance of being able to receive: receiving help, receiving love, receiving support. Receiving is indeed a double blessing; in the receiving we were also giving. We were giving others an opportunity to contribute, the opportunity to be included in this journey together, to show their kindness and caring. Community can and needs to be reciprocal of giving and receiving; appreciating, sharing gratitude, sharing joy, and sharing sorrow.

Community reminds us that we do not exist in isolation. The whole is much more than the sum of its parts. Together, we can reach farther and accomplish so much more when each individual is doing their part in support of a common goal. We are each strengthened and able to do more than we might believe is possible when we are connected within ourselves, as well as being open to receiving support from others.

THE JOURNEY TOWARDS THE SUMMIT

The example that comes to mind is my experience of the Ride2Survive - a cycling trip of 400 km from Kelowna to Delta in just one day to raise funds for cancer research and treatment. Now, if anyone had told me that I would be doing this ride in the midst of being a new mother with a husband who was still going through the last of his cancer treatments, and that he would be doing this ride together with me, I would have laughed at the idea that it was even possible. But the strength of the human spirit — that mighty will that shows up when determined to defy all odds and that still, quiet voice that whispers "Well, let's try and see what happens" — was stronger than my belief and prevailed in the decision to undertake this epic journey.

The decision that was made cued community's arrival. Those people who champion your efforts and lift you up in support and encouragement. The training together, the supporting one another, the rallying together in their own private journey and unique reasons for doing this ride intricately weaved a web of community around us. Going through the moments of working towards something that we really believed in and knew from first-hand experience to be worth all the fight and effort.

One of the many poignant memories I have from that ride was my experience of cycling the Penask Summit; a long, gruelling, gradual climb out of Kelowna. I had already decided that I would not complete that climb — after all, I had all kinds of excuses and reasons and it was perfectly fine with my plan to just stop and take a break in one of the support vehicles once I got too tired of pushing up that hill. However, that plan was not meant to happen. The magic that can unfold in containers sometimes has very different plans from our own. I reached the ruthless point when my legs felt like lead and I could barely pedal onward. I was truly ready to give up. I honestly felt okay with how far I had managed to climb considering I was never planning to do the whole summit anyway. In fact, I had already surprised myself by going farther than originally anticipated. Somewhere in the exhaustion of leg muscles and the slight satisfaction of being ready to stop, I felt the slight touch of a hand on my back. It is amazing how the slightest touch of someone else's hand while they cycle beside you can ease each pedal stroke, as though they were actually pushing you up the hill. This small gesture was a physical relief but it also represented something bigger; the encouragement and belief others had that I could actually climb that summit. At that moment, they — my cycling community — believed in me more than I believed in myself. Had I been on my own, I guarantee I would have stopped when I was tired, believing I could go no further. And then I reminded myself of what had helped me get through the past year of going through the journey of cancer with my husband: focusing on taking things moment by moment. Suddenly, I stopped wondering how much farther and how distant the summit seemed and literally took one pedal-stroke at a time, admired the amazing views, and got into my "zone." When Rod and I both reached the summit, it was exhilarating and quite symbolic of our own respective journeys. In fact, the whole Ride2Survive profoundly taught me that when we are supporting one another, cheering each other on, providing strength for one another whether it be in physical, mental, emotional or spiritual form, we are much more powerful together than in isolation. There is an alchemy of connecting with the strength and resources within ourselves, and allowing others' strengths and resources to provide support to take us beyond where we could have imagined.

QUESTIONS FOR REFLECTION

1. **Think of the various communities you have been a part of throughout your life and list them here.**

    For example: Extended family, church or religious community, school community, the community of sports teams or extracurricular activities you were a part of, clubs, volunteering, choirs, peer groups, and so on.

2. **What are some adjectives you would use to describe the positive and negative qualities of each of these communities? Find qualities for each one of the communities that you listed.**

    For example: Extended family — loyal, caring, loving, opinionated, strong-willed, placating at times.

    Music community — fun, playful, eager to learn and perform, unique and diverse members, sometimes competitive

    School community — competitive, loyalty within peer groups, creative, cliquish, sometimes judgmental and opinionated

    Continue listing each community and describe their positive and negative qualities.

3. **How have each of these communities contributed to who you are today?**

    For example: As I reflect on each of the communities that I have been involved in, I believe that many of them have contributed to my sense of belonging and loyalty. At times, especially when I was younger, my desire to belong and fit in would come at a cost to myself, as I would sometimes conform in order to be accepted. Now that I am older, I notice that I am part of communities that value and grow from differences and encourage collaborative sharing of ideas.

    My values of service to others and contributing to the bigger picture of cultivating more peace and love in the world have also been developed within some of these communities.

4. **What kind of community do you wish to cultivate in your present life? Think of who you would like to be around more and what is it about them that you are drawn to?**

    For example: I would like to make time to more consciously cultivate the time and space needed for connection within community. I would like to actively engage in activities that feed my life energy alongside others who have a sense of vitality and interests that stimulate my learning and growth. (Be specific about what this could look like: what particular activities, name specific people who either are already part of your community or whom you would like to be more connected with in community.)

5. **What decision are you making right now about how you will actively create, cultivate, and/or participate in your community?**

For example: I will reach out to connect more personally with individuals to cultivate a deeper overall connection with my community. I will volunteer to help with some of the work of the group and show up ready to collaborate and share ideas. I will find a club or group that meets regularly to engage in a shared interest (such as music, art, hiking, or any activity that feeds your soul).

Spirituality is recognizing that we are all inextricably connected to one another by a power greater than all of us, and that **our connection** to that power and to one another is grounded in **love** and **compassion**.

- Brené Brown

14

The Universal Container

How do we cultivate the container within us, the container between us, and the container among us? Are we a part of the container, creating the container, or is it more a combination of the two?

Perhaps it is even much, much bigger than that being that we are all part of the vastness and expansiveness of this universe. Each one of us is unique and different with nobody else being exactly the same, and yet we are all part of the bigger picture that when woven together, creates the tapestry of all creation and humanity. So how does this translate to how we contribute to this planet and to one another? Do we choose to be passive recipients or active participants in our lives? Do we experience ourselves as stars or as supporting roles in the stories of our life? And, if we choose to fully experience ourselves and others in our lives, we need to also look at how we will shine and support others in shining their own light. We can support one another standing as individuals in our uniqueness, and as parts of the greater whole in our connectedness.

THE BARRIERS AND OBSTACLES THAT WE CREATE

On a practical level, this means removing barriers and obstacles. When it comes right down to it, the majority of barriers and obstacles that get in our way are of our own creation — emotional blocks, psychic barriers, perceptual snares, rigid and sticky expectations to name a few of the popular ones. As a species, we are extremely resourceful: we build protective barriers as we see fit for our survival. Why do we want so desperately to survive? Because, I believe, on some cellular level we know that we are here to contribute in some way. We are born to grow, to learn, to evolve, to make some kind of difference that will have an impact; whether it impacts one life, many lives, a community, or this planet. Ultimately it is not about the quantity of our impacts but the quality. We are seduced by the spell of the ripple effect, knowing that impacting even one life will ripple outward to energetically impact many. This is true both for when we are loving and compassionate, and also when we are judging and dispassionate. What kind of a world do we want to live in? However you answer that question, the next step is asking yourself what your own unique part is in creating that world.

The difference between being an active participant in Life or a passive recipient of whatever is thrown your way is in how you answer that question. If you want to live in a technicolour, multi-dimensional, experiential, connected, loving, accepting, growth-oriented world, then you had better well do your part by living a technicolour, multi-dimensional, experiential, connected, loving, accepting, growth-oriented life. This means embracing all of it — the multi-faceted aspects of all of your experience, which includes the devastation, the joy, the fear, the grief, the happiness, the despair and everything in between. It means

158

going through it and trusting that there is light at the end of the tunnels of despair. And yes, sometimes it means wallowing in it until you find a way to move through it. Wallowing has its purpose as long as you do not stay in the wallowing and forget to move. Living all of your experience means leaping and dancing when you are in your joy, crying when you are in your sadness, trembling when you are in your fear. Embrace all of it! Living each precious present moment, learning from the moment, and then living some more.

MOMENTS OF AWE

Fully showing up for your life also means allowing yourself to be captivated by moments of awe. It requires you to take a closer look at the magic of it all. Really, this world is a magical place and you, yourself are rather magical and miraculous. It is amazing — almost unbelievable — that every one of us literally has a whole universe within us: we each hold one hundred billion neurons and there are one hundred billion stars in the universe. Is that a coincidence? If it is, it is truly an amazing one. Taking in the awe of life is truly awe-some. Awe is that feeling you get when you are in the presence of something vast. It is not about the scale, it is about the quality. It is literally and metaphorically like when you finally get to the summit of that mountain and the view is so stunningly beautiful and breathtaking. An awe-filled experience is when you are filled with emotion and joy at the wonder and vastness of a moment.

Moments of awe can change the course of your life in profound and permanent ways. These moments are not only about the joys but also about the devastation. Both are vast, both are bigger than you alone, and both connect you in miraculous ways.

Those moments can be experienced alone, in relationship, or in community, in the witnessing and "withnessing" of another's experience. For it is in the witnessing of the experience that the experience itself shifts and changes. When I am with another as they are in their pain and devastation or as they are with me in mine, we are not alone. In our connection, our sharing of the moment, the experience is no longer the same. It may still be tragic, devastating, sad, frustrating and fearful, but there is something about having another human being present that can provide moments of comfort and connection, even within the moments of utmost despair.

The universal container offers us opportunities at every turn to lose ourselves in feeling connected to the oneness of it all. To allow ourselves to be awed. To allow ourselves to connect with that much, much bigger container that holds each and every one of us. That something is far greater than what can be fully understood.

QUESTIONS FOR REFLECTION

1. **What are some moments of awe that you have had?**

It could be as small as watching a caterpillar work across a leaf, its tiny legs slowly inching it forward, or as grand as a beautiful vista, or more humanly connected in witnessing a birth, or feeling a hand reach out for yours when you didn't know you needed it. There can be a whole range of these moments and they don't need to be earth-shattering.

2. **Choose one of these moments to focus on and journal about your experience of awe.**

3. **What does it mean to you to be a part of the universal container?**

When we are more **accepting, compassionate, grateful**, and **loving** in our lives we are doing our part to bring **peace** into the world.
- Jennifer Nagel

15

The Great Container

When we take a moment to truly reflect on the Universal container that holds space for every one of us on this planet, we need to consider what our part is in this Great Container of our human experience. We are each responsible for finding our own still point within, discovering and creating our own safety and refuge within ourselves, to form our own unique container. When I reflect on our unique containers — consisting of the space within ourselves, the space between us and others, and the space among all — I picture Russian nesting dolls. You may know those wooden dolls that come apart to reveal another doll inside, which has yet another doll within it, until you reach the tiniest doll at the heart of the last one. Each doll is held within a larger doll, the same way our own individual container nestles within the container of our relationships with others, which nestles in the container of community, which nestles in the container of culture, humanity, and the ultimate Container that goes beyond our universe.

Connecting to the container within ourselves — our unique container — cultivates a place within us to both witness and participate in our experience on all levels including physically, mentally, emotionally and spiritually. We can allow ourselves to go to the depths and seek out the shadows, the light, and everything in between. Seeking out the shadows means to acknowledge and honour every part of us including the parts that we perceive as negative and ugly. Those parts that, when they emerge, we may wish it were possible to simply erase, rewind, and hit the reset button a little sooner within ourselves. However, by seeking out the shadows and allowing ourselves to see them, they can be allowed to transform by the very fact that they are no longer in darkness. Our relationship with these different parts of ourselves can shift and change when we can acknowledge and appreciate what they are trying to do to support or protect us, even when sometimes falling short of their intentions.

There is a dance that takes place between the space you hold within yourself and your experience, and the space within the larger whole that includes others. We all impact one another. When you accept and love yourself, you extend those same qualities to others through relationships and then beyond out into the world. When you radiate love and acceptance out into the world you are also activating your caring, compassion and kindness. These are the gifts available for each one of us to both give and receive. The world truly changes when we bring more love and acceptance to ourselves, others, and all living things on this planet.

The container is so much bigger than you or me. It is not driven by ego or bound by our physical bodies. It is an energy. I experience this energy within myself and also from a source much bigger than me, that is more difficult to describe. How I use this energy or how I choose to connect with it has an impact on how I respond to what is in front of me. It shows in whether I react to the driver who cut me off in traffic or I just take a breath, send out some love and acceptance, and carry on. Whether I yell at my children to stop fighting, or slow things down and really listen with my heart to what each one of them is experiencing.

While we can get caught up in the muck and messiness of life sometimes, the muck also gives us an opportunity to find the magic within it when we allow ourselves to slow down and make a conscious decision to get through this. Within the muck we can continue to work on our own containers of acceptance and love. Perhaps the lesson is that it's necessary to acknowledge the muck — the grime, the grit, and the messy parts of life — while at the same time cultivating more acceptance and love within the container. When we are more accepting, compassionate, grateful, and loving in our lives we are doing our part to bring peace into the world. We cultivate a state of mind, heart, and soul that allows us to see the wondrous parts of Creation overall, even within the muck that certainly does not feel wondrous when we are in the thick of it. When we respond with love and compassion we start to see what really matters in life and the bigger picture becomes clearer.

THE BIG PICTURE

I had a peculiar dream one night that held a scene of a vast ocean in the Arctic with many icebergs. The beauty of these magnificent structures of ice rising from the water was striking. Knowing how much larger and deeper these structures go beneath the waterline, I was reminded of Satir's iceberg metaphor that depicts how much more there is going on beneath the surface of what we see in human behaviours. Beneath the water line is a whole depth of internal experience with our emotional world, our beliefs and perceptions, our expectations — of ourselves and others — our deep yearnings and with the essence of who we are at our core. In the same way that there is nobody else on earth exactly like you, there is no iceberg exactly like another. Every one is unique. And yet all icebergs come from the same source: water. When an iceberg melts it simply returns to its original form of water and is one with the ocean. In the same way, we all come from the same source and yet our lives are manifested in unique ways. We are all connected and yet we are also separate from one another.

There is a well-known style of Chinese carving called the Family Ball that involves intricate spheres within spheres within spheres, all carved from one solid piece of jade or wood. The artist progresses from the inside out and each sphere has beautiful, elaborate, designs carved on it. The spheres symbolize love and represent the various generations of one's family. Each sphere moves independently within the next larger sphere. They are separate, yet part of the greater whole and all come from the same single source of material, again reminding us that we are connected as individuals and part of something so much bigger.

As I reflect on the interconnectivity and oneness of life, I look out over the water at the mountains and I can see them as separate — the water separating the land over there from the land over here. Yet when I consider the bigger picture, I imagine following those mountains down to the bottom of the water, where the land continues along and rises again to the land on the other side. The Earth's surface is filled with rises and falls, peaks and valleys, cliffs, drop-offs, crevices, and fissures. Some of these are filled with bodies of water that separate the land into its various masses and islands. They are also separate, and yet deeply connected and part of the whole of this Earth.

What Does It All Mean?

If everything and everyone is connected and part of the whole, then we need to question what our responsibilities are and what our part is in, and for, this whole. Embracing the mystery and the miracle of that connection fills me with awe and inspires me to live more fully, to have compassion for humanity, and to do my part — to uphold my responsibility. To contribute, I desire to cultivate more connection, more love, more acceptance, more understanding, more joy, and more freedom. In practical terms this means practicing this in my daily life with all whom I contact. It means being easier on myself when I mess it up. It means going easier on others when they mess it up. That may look the same for you, as you also offer what you are able in connection with your part of the whole. It means we must be open to seeing those moments of grace.

STEWARDSHIP: WHAT DOES THAT LOOK LIKE FOR YOU?

What's in it for you if you were to live intentionally in all areas of your life? That would ask that you be intentional in how you cultivate the containers of your life: the one within your Self - that still point of peace, acceptance and love; the one between that holds the space of your relationships with others and leads to your cultivation and connection with the container that holds community; and all the many parts of what contributes to that sense of being part of something so much bigger. Living intentionally and being more conscious of the moments of your life allows you to be more responsible for your own experience and to cultivate the gift of sovereignty over the choices you make in each moment of your life. In nurturing the containers of your life, you are also opening yourself to more freedom and joy. Once you do bring that intentionality, what is in it for you?

My sense is that we are all wanting to grow and learn, to let go of old patterns and to make way for new, more life-giving ways of being. In doing so, we impart the gift of our own healing and growth to the next generation. When we choose love, acceptance, belonging and connection, the impact on every part of our life is far different than were we to choose hate, intolerance, exclusion and isolation.

"The conducting, supervising, or managing of something; especially the careful and responsible management of something entrusted to one's care" is the Merriam-Webster dictionary definition of stewardship. We have all been given such a beautiful gift, but with that gift comes responsibility. Remember that the whole is greater than the sum of its parts. While we are whole as human beings, we are also merely a part of something bigger. How you choose to responsibly manage and care for your Self, others, and this Earth - to steward — is entirely up to you.

LEAD BY FOLLOWING, FOLLOW BY LEADING

Let's look at leadership for a moment and shift from a hierarchical "top-down" model of leadership to a more "equality of value" growth model, learning to lead by following. Following the energy to determine and intuit what needs to happen moment by moment.

Learning to use the signals, the hints, the confrontations, the body sensations, and ultimately, to just be yourself. In the work that I do, my job is to keep a group's energy channeled in positive, creative directions. I listen to the sensations within me to guide my decisions of where we go next. If my heart is pounding and there is a nervous energy flowing through me, I know I need to do something to slow down the process of the group, to get back on track, to get someone out of their story and into their experience. If I have the desire to yawn or go to sleep, I know I need to do something to shift the energy, through movement, stretching, guided meditation, dancing or anything to change the flow. Leading by following does not mean that we are blindly led by others. If we can hold onto the bigger picture of where we are going, where it is we are leading, we can allow ourselves to also be fully present to what is happening right in front of and around us. If I am leading, I am still in charge of the process but those who are following are in charge of what comes into the space at any moment in time. My clients are in charge of deciding what they want to have different in their lives. My job is to help them with the "how." In leading by following we are both engaged in co-creating the process. We are on this journey of change and transformation together. We become synchronized in our leading and following. I am leading by following the cues of the followers. They are following by leading their desired change. We are both leading and following, flowing together in an energetic dance towards healing.

THE BIGGER PICTURE

The whole picture suddenly becomes clear: honour the space within ourselves, the space between through our relationships, and among us in our communities, our cultures, and our whole world. When we can bring more love to ourselves, to others and to the world we also do our part by contributing to a more beautiful reality. Honouring the space is to acknowledge, to love, and to protect.

* Acknowledging your own unique Self and connecting with that space within you that is peace, that is love, and that is stillness.
* Acknowledging the spaces between in your relationships — that unique energy that exists between you and another person and how you respond to that energy.
* Acknowledging the spaces among all of humanity and our living world.

To honour, to love, and to protect all of these spaces within the containers is what I think might be stewardship; the way to take responsibility for the opportunity and gift of being born into this beautiful and messy world. It is how we contribute to the development of ourselves, our families, our communities, our cultures, our world, and our universe. For it is in experiencing ourselves in these intricate connections and spaces between that we can truly show up — not only for ourselves, but for Life and all that it entails, including those moments of grace.

When I look back at the moments of my life, I can see where Grace was present. Grace was very much there through my husband's challenging battle with cancer, through a burgeoning community of support, through a deep willingness by Rod and me to show up, through every sacred moment of reprieve from the chaos, and through the many miracles that showed up in various forms. I have this reminder every morning when Rod makes me coffee and brings it to my bedside. But this is not the only moment of grace in my day. I see them everywhere now, from the eagle soaring high above me to remind me of the bigger picture when I am mired in the maze of an overwhelming to-do list, to the stranger who offers to lift my heavy suitcase for me, to the sounds of laughter coming from my children.

All the various containers that hold my experience offer me moments of grace. Within myself they arrive in moments of amazement such as when I witness my body changing with age; in my relationships — the container between — there are moments of shared joy when my daughter overcomes a fear of dogs or when a client dares to find their own voice; equally, when we share a moment of loss or experiencing our humanity like I did on that fateful bus trip in Peru; moments of grace among community such as being able to offer organizational skills with compassion and care, and knowing how deeply community is impacted by those who understand and have a shared vision. These moments of grace allow for truth and joy to radiate from inside, like that of the sunshine that follows rain. Each of those connection points — within, between, and among — has the potential for us to experience a moment of grace. Some of them are indeed more difficult, yet they all invite us more fully into being, to make the most of our gifts and no matter the circumstance, to be bestowed with a precious moment of grace.

FINAL REFLECTION

Imagine for a moment that you have in front of you a beautiful book that contains the story of your life so far. If you were to open the book to a brand new page, the page of today and this moment in time, what words or images would you put there? And just notice all the pages that have already been filled on one side, your history to this moment in time, and so many blank pages on the other side that have yet to be filled with all the experiences that are still to come in your life with all of their learnings that you will gain.

We do not need to go backwards in the book. Sometimes we can be curious and want to return and remember something, but we are not going to read the old book over and over again. We are going to stay with the new pages and add to them starting today. I wonder what you would write in that book today; what your hopes and wishes would be for this day — not for the whole rest of your life but just for this day. How will you show up for your life today?

Now imagine what your experience would be like if you were already there living your hopes and wishes — what it would be like, how you would feel, how you would see yourself and others, what your expectations of yourself might be and how you might be fulfilling your yearnings differently. How would you connect with that deepest part of yourself if you created what you wrote in your book? If you can imagine it, you are already beginning to create it. You deserve love, acceptance, peace, safety, connection, belonging, intimacy, freedom; you deserve to be important in your own life. See if you are willing to appreciate those beautiful yearnings that are there to remind you of your place in this universe, the legacy that you inherit just by being human. Your connection to all that is. What do you want to add? Maybe you need to be more loving to yourself, or more loving to others. Or maybe you need to be more open to receiving love and acceptance, opening your heart to really let life in. Can you be more accepting of yourself, including your vulnerable parts, more accepting of others, and more accepting of what you experience regardless of the context?

Whatever your yearnings are, see if you are willing to allow yourself to decide what you would like to have. Change is possible for anyone. Change is possible for the world. Change. You can be in charge of your change. You can be in charge of what you want. You can be in charge of how you change and who you invite to change with you. Your change belongs to you.

Epilogue

Life is always showing up for us, but we are not always showing up for Life. We all have our own unique stories and experiences. Not a single person on this planet has had the exact same experiences in the sequence and context that you have lived. You truly are the star of your own life. And yet there are some universal lessons to be learned in these unique experiences. Some universal lessons show up disguised as teachers in the people we meet, the parents we are born to, the places we see, and the work we choose to do. Universal lessons about living, loving, letting go, transforming, connecting, dying, belonging, freedom, independence and dependence. These are listed in no particular order for Life is cyclical, circular, and non-linear. Even at birth we begin learning about independence as soon as the umbilical cord is severed. Lessons of dependence and survival, and of how we learn to get our basic needs met, follow rapidly. Our teachers for life are everywhere, including those who catalyze conflict or difficulty. Maybe even especially among those with whom we feel confronted. If we avoid it, whether it's a discussion or a dynamic, we miss the lesson. There are no short cuts. The lesson will come again. There are no quick fixes. No magic elixir to get straight to paradise, bypassing all tragedy, sorrow, grief and loss. The most beautiful aspect is that we can look for the gems in each and every one of our stories. We can discover and connect with our gifts and resources that have helped us get this far in Life. Whether you write your story as protagonist or victim, star or anonymous bystander, is your choice. Everyone has a story of loss. Everyone has stories of tragedy, connection, awe, fear, and injustice. And every single one of us has Stories of Grace.

Acknowledgements

Writing this book has been a thrilling adventure for me where I have learned that it really takes a whole community to bring it all to fruition. I would like to thank some of the amazing people who have contributed in their unique ways.

To all my friends and colleagues who ever told me "you should write a book," thank you for planting that seed even when I had no inkling of what kind of book I would write.

To my wonderful husband Rod, thank you for the adventure that is our life together, for loving me and for all the ways that you supported me in the writing of this book. There is nobody I would rather journey through and out of the muck with than you. Thanks for the magic!

To my parents, who go way above and beyond the call of duty in the areas of childcare so that I can do the work that I do. You have always paved the way to support my dreams and this book certainly would not have been written without the countless ways you have supported me. I am profoundly thankful for you both.

Big thanks to my editor extraordinaire, Karen Melin, who was beyond amazing at truly "getting" me. You have such a gift of slowing everything down to get to the juicy heart of what really wants to be written. Thank you for your belief in my abilities as a writer, for helping me get the words out and for your enthusiastic support of the message of this book.

To my publisher, Julie Salisbury, thank you for your enthusiastic "yes" to this manuscript and for going above and beyond my expectations in your support for this project. What a great adventure this has been!

I am forever grateful for the teachings of Virginia Satir. Her vision for "peace within, peace between, and peace among" has always resonated with me greatly and it is a privilege for me to teach her model of growth and transformation throughout the world.

To Dr. John Banmen, thank you for introducing me to Satir Transformational Systemic Therapy in my graduate school days and continuing to mentor and teach me over these past 20 years.

Thank you Kathlyne Maki-Banmen for believing in my abilities before I believed in them myself. I am grateful for your mentorship over the years and teaching me the art of facilitation and group process.

Huge thanks to my dear friend Linda Lucas in Idaho, USA whose words of wisdom and support have been such a gift to me. I am so grateful for your friendship and for all of your honest feedback not only on this book, but in all areas of life too.

To Dr. Carolyn Nesbitt, thank you so much for your enthusiasm, your encouragement and your friendship. Your willingness to read through the entire manuscript with your skilled eyes and open heart helped me to forge ahead with this project.

I am also profoundly grateful for all of my clients and group participants over the years. You have all been my teachers in many ways — thank you for your vulnerability, your trust, and for the gift of witnessing your journey out of the muck and into the magic of your life.

About The Author

Born in Vancouver, BC, Canada, **Jennifer Nagel, MA, RCC** studied Psychology in University and found that the best learning came from life experience and doing the work she is so passionate about. She writes about the process of change from first-hand experience of emerging from 'the muck' and she has helped many others on their journeys of learning to show up more fully for their lives.

Jennifer is a Registered Clinical Counsellor and works with individuals, couples and families. She travels the world and teaches both professional and personal growth programs in Canada, China and Kenya. She works with a diversity of groups including therapists, educators, school programs, community groups, at-risk adolescents, therapeutic programs, non-profit organizations and corporate groups.

Jennifer is a member of the British Columbia Association for Clinical Counsellors, the International Family Therapy Association, the Virginia Satir Global Network and a clinical member of the Satir Institute of the Pacific. She is also the Director of Training for the Satir Institute of the Pacific and a senior trainer and faculty for the Banmen Satir China Management Centre. Jennifer works with individuals, couples, families and youth in private practice, and provides clinical supervision to other therapists. She is passionate about teaching Satir Transformational Systemic Therapy programs around the world and helping others to re-connect with the magic of who they truly are.

www.jennifernagelcounselling.com

www.magicinthemuck.com

jennifernagel1@yahoo.com

Resources

For more information on training and resources related to Transformational Systemic Therapy and the Satir Model:

Satir Institute of the Pacific

www.satirpacific.org

For more information about the global network of institutes and affiliates:

Virginia Satir Global Network

www.satirglobal.org

For more information about the grassroots cancer fundraising project of the Ride2Survive:

Ride2Survive

www.ride2survive.ca

References in the book to the Iceberg Metaphor and the Satir Model:

Satir, V., Banmen, J., Gerber, J., & Gomori, M. 1991. The Satir Model: Family Therapy and Beyond. Palo Alto, CA: Science and Behavior Books. Inc.